Anatomy of an Actor

Jack Nicholson

Beverly Walker

Introduction   6

1   George Hanson   16
        Easy Rider (1969)
        Dennis Hopper

2   Robert "Bobby" Eroica Dupea   32
        Five Easy Pieces (1970)
        Bob Rafelson

3   J. J. "Jake" Gittes   48
        Chinatown (1974)
        Roman Polanski

4   Randle Patrick McMurphy   64
        One Flew Over the Cuckoo's Nest (1975)
        Miloš Forman

5   Jack Torrance   80
        The Shining (1980)
        Stanley Kubrick

6   Jack Napier, a.k.a. The Joker   98
        Batman (1989)
        Tim Burton

7   Colonel Nathan R. Jessep   112
        A Few Good Men (1992)
        Rob Reiner

8   Melvin Udall   126
        As Good As It Gets (1997)
        James L. Brooks

9   Warren Schmidt   140
        About Schmidt (2002)
        Alexander Payne

10 Harry Sanborn   154
        Something's Gotta Give (2003)
        Nancy Meyers

        Conclusion   169
        Chronology   173
        Filmography   177
        Bibliography   185
        Notes   186
        Index   190

Introduction

"My first acting teacher said all art is one thing—a stimulating point of departure. That's it. And if you can do that in a piece, you've fulfilled your cultural, sociological obligation as a workman."[1]
—Jack Nicholson

Rebel. Clown. Satyr. Devil. If Jack Nicholson were an edifice, he'd have a firm foundation, solid walls, and gargoyle-like embellishments around the top. The building would be known for its wicked little demons, just as the actor is cherished for his most outlandish roles: the grinning madman of *The Shining* (1980), the disfigured Joker in *Batman* (1989), the devil himself in *The Witches of Eastwick* (1987).

To this gallery of monsters one might add a dim-witted thug (*Prizzi's Honor*, 1985), a werewolf (*Wolf*, 1994), and even a snappish Marine officer (*A Few Good Men*, 1992), through whom the actor supplied a maxim for the times: "You can't handle the truth!"

None of these portraits brought him an Oscar, but they're the ones the average moviegoer thinks of first. Stardom is evanescent, sustainable only by the audience. When a repairman in my home noticed the actor's name on books and articles scattered about, he said with great enthusiasm, "Jack Nicholson is a wild man! Wild!" After I assured him the actor wasn't really "wild" but a serious craftsman, he said, "Oh, he's good; he's always good. I know that." And then he spoke about one of Nicholson's lesser known films, *The Pledge* (2001), in which he plays a retired cop confused by the civilian world he has reentered. "I sometimes feel just like him," the repairman said, emulating a moment when the character turns round and round, gazing in bewilderment at the tree-filled sky.

That in a nutshell speaks to the genius of Jack Nicholson: his extraordinary talent for communicating the nexus of emotion—hopes, dreams, fears, sorrows—his character is experiencing. Strong men tremble. The most erudite critic can feel defeated by Nicholson's ability to pierce his detachment and enter his heart. Richard Schickel, Stanley Kauffmann, and Roger Ebert are three distinguished American critics who have admitted in print to being brought to tears by Nicholson's performances as Schmidt (*About Schmidt*, 2002), Hoffa (*Hoffa*, 1992), and Bobby Dupea (*Five Easy Pieces*, 1970).

Women also admire Nicholson, but differently. We retain a degree of understandable ambivalence, given the way his characters have treated females in so many films. As a star of the first magnitude, he had the luxury of choice, and he chose male-centric stories about fractured, tormented, and compromised men. It's his "satirical approach to macho,"[2] as critic Pauline Kael called it, that helps him escape our wrath. As in life, women see through the character's braggadocio to the trembling soul beneath; and while we aren't on his wavelength like men, we appreciate his fine-drawn portraits, his charm and charisma. When he displays a tad of romantic vulnerability or mere decency, as in *Terms of Endearment* (1983) and *Something's Gotta Give* (2003), we are touched.

Jack Nicholson is unique to his era. No screen actor has taken greater risks in his choice of material; none has pushed the performance envelope more often in style or content; none has a credit list so diverse—and yet none has enjoyed more official recognition. He has been nominated a record twelve times for an Academy Award, at least once in every decade, and won three Oscars along with countless other accolades, including a Kennedy Center Honor in 2001. He's a walking contradiction, often taking supporting roles even after he became a star, and lowering his astronomical fee for projects and people who are especially meaningful to him. "Jack chooses the role, not its importance in the story. He picks his directors carefully and is brilliant at knowing the talented from the not,"[3] said Bob Rafelson, who directed Nicholson in six films—more than anyone else. Rafelson and his partner, the late Bert Schneider, played a crucial role in Nicholson's early career, seeing to it that he was cast in *Easy Rider* (1969) and then executive producing, along with Steve Blauner, his directorial debut film, *Drive, He Said* (1971).

Jack Nicholson delights an audience like no other dramatic actor. He has an uncanny ability to elicit laughter out of the most dicey or improbable situations, and could have turned his career toward comedy had he cared to. Voted class clown in high school, he has always enjoyed being *baaaad*—or pretending to be. His expressive,

Top: Jack at 18 during his first year in California, 1955.

Bottom: The Nicholson family — Lorraine (left), Ethel May (center), Jack and June (right) — and friends.

mobile face can move from charming and friendly to menacing and malevolent in a matter of seconds—and no one can wiggle his eyebrows so meaningfully as Nicholson. He isn't vain about his appearance and has done little to protect his private life. In fact, he has been all too willing to entertain the press with talk about sex, girlfriends, monogamy aversion, and marijuana, among other juicy topics. "I resist all established beliefs. My religion basically is to be immediate, to live in the now. It's an old cliché, I know, but it's mine,"[4] he gleefully states as his working philosophy.

This devil-may-care image served a strategic purpose for Nicholson during the hedonistic 1970s. Chatter about free love and drugs made good copy and kept his name in headlines—not only with the public but also with potential producers who might offer him a role. But as the devastating effects of drug use became evident and the AIDS epidemic gained momentum, it led to a confusion of realms. People within the film industry as well as critics, the media, and the public began to believe his entertaining balderdash. He became more cautious, occasionally saying plaintively that many things written about him weren't true.

The persona Nicholson has projected his entire life might be the result of a habit left over from childhood—a need to disguise, or at least fudge, what a serious man he really is—"smart about being smart,"[5] as his friend Harry Gittes put it. As a kid, he hid his report card from classmates so they wouldn't see the A's. A's weren't cool. A's would separate him from the group, confer an elite status that he did not wish to have. Now that he is seventy-six, most people know he is a natural intellectual, brimming with curiosity, who is widely read and traveled. He bridles at being treated like a monument by younger actors glowing in his presence, and he can still toss out an expletive or two—to show he's "one of the guys." These are some of the travails of a man who has been at the pinnacle of his profession for nearly half a century. He might yearn to be just like you and me, but he isn't.

Life Upside Down

By 1974, Nicholson had received four Oscar nominations. His star was in the ascendant, and his every quip, pronouncement, or outrage, verbal or otherwise, made it into the papers. He felt like James Cagney in *White Heat* (1949): "Made it, Ma. Top o' the world!" Then the telephone rang. An editor from *Time* magazine was on the other end with a tale too strange for fiction. While researching the actor's background for a cover story, they'd inadvertently uncovered a Nicholson family secret. To wit, the two people he had always regarded as his parents were actually his grandparents; his biological mother was his elder sister, June. Nicholson was thirty-seven years old

at the time. He had been married and divorced, and he had a daughter, Jennifer.

It's easy to imagine the disorienting effect of this revelation, the torrent of emotions that swept over him, made all the more acute because both women were by then deceased—June at the young age of forty-four. This left him without an opportunity to reconcile the two realities and learn the identity of his biological father. Fortunately, his aunt Lorraine and her husband, George "Shorty" Smith, were able to fill in some of the gaps. With time, he recovered his balance and in 2004 responded to *Playboy* magazine's nosy questions. "I came to feel only gratitude. [...] [T]here were certain things about my relationship with [June] that were clarified when I learned the truth. Just small things, body English. Your mother relates to you differently than your sister does. [...] I remember thinking, when my sister doted on me, What are you worried about? But of course a mother would worry. [...] [O]thers must have kept the secret, too. [...] I grew up in a very small town [but] never heard an inkling about this. [...] It doesn't matter. I had a great family situation there."[6]

The Jersey Shore

Born April 22, 1937, Jack Nicholson grew up near New Jersey's beautiful Atlantic seacoast, in the towns of Neptune, Manasquan, and Asbury Park.

Ethel May Nicholson, his grandmother, operated a successful beauty salon from her home. As the business thrived, "Mud," as she was known, moved into more affluent areas with excellent schools. She and her husband, John Joseph Nicholson, after whom the actor is named, had two daughters, June and Lorraine. Although Ethel was reared a Protestant, she adopted her husband's Catholic faith upon marriage and raised the children in an observant—but not pious—environment.

Though Jack's grandparents informally separated around the time of his birth, he had contact with John Joseph Nicholson. He remembers him fondly as a sharp dresser—a man with style who'd once had a successful career as a window dresser for upscale department stores. "Jake Gittes's get-up is after that man, who was very natty," says Nicholson of his character in *Chinatown*. "I've used him a lot actually—for a man I didn't see much. The glasses in *Easy Rider* were the same type he wore."[7]

A spirit of creativity permeated the Nicholson household. Ethel was a skilled seamstress and amateur painter. June studied dance and made her public debut at age seven. She began dancing professionally while still in her teens and left home when Jack was four to become an Earl Carroll showgirl in Miami.

Jack attended Roosevelt Grammar School and made his own show biz debut at age ten,

singing "Managua, Nicaragua." He managed the sports teams and appeared in school, church, and community plays and other performing events. At Manasquan High School he was such an excellent student that he skipped a grade. A few months after his high school graduation, he left for California with borrowed coin. The year was 1954. He was seventeen.

Show Biz

"Jack has always known where he was going, always thought of himself as a star, and has never changed the way he thinks about himself,"[8] according to Monte Hellman, who worked with Nicholson early in his career.

Though the teen had never articulated a specific goal in life, he immediately gravitated to the movie world, snaring a job in the cartoon department at MGM. He was befriended by famous animators Bill Hanna and Joe Barbera, who suggested he apprentice at the Players Ring theater, which he did. He began to study acting, first with Jeff Corey and then with Martin Landau. He also took roles in small theater productions, though he felt a decided preference for cinema from the start. Nicholson might be the only star of his era without strong theater roots.

Landau was persuaded to teach a class at the Dahl Theater by Monte Hellman, a stage director who would soon play a significant role in Nicholson's professional life. Landau—who won an Academy Award for the film *Ed Wood* (1994), directed by Tim Burton—remembers the young Jack Nicholson very well. "He had great teeth and a shock of hair; he was charming, funny, smart—and serious." Landau thought he "avoided a certain kind of emotion, using instead his charm," and prescribed a series of exercises to free the actor's inner child. "I try to infuse an actor with a sense of play—to accept something he feels and go there. Our imaginations are rich; we tend to short-circuit them."[9] Nicholson even now continues to practice some of these exercises.

In a "birds of a feather" way, Nicholson naturally fell in with an underground community of actors, writers, and directors whose sensibilities were at odds with the calcified mainstream film industry. A decade would pass before a desperate industry would throw open its doors and beg them enter; meantime, they took whatever jobs came their way on the margins of the establishment. Nicholson vividly remembers how thrilled he was to be cast in *The Cry Baby Killer* (1958)—and then not work again for nine months.

King of the B's filmmaker-producer Roger Corman and Monte Hellman were the two most important figures in Nicholson's professional life during the 1960s. It was hard for Nicholson to get roles, and he became legitimately discouraged about his chances of making it as an actor. He began writing screenplays, by himself and with Hellman. Their first effort, *Epitaph*, was about abortion, a forbidden subject, and it never got off the ground. "I thought Jack should direct and told him so," said Hellman. "He always exhibited an overall interest in the project—in its totality, not just from the perspective of being an actor."[10] Nicholson wrote a second script, *Flight to Fury* (1964), which he and Hellman made back-to-back in the Philippines with *Back Door to Hell* (1964). Eighteen months later, they used the same configuration for two Westerns made in Utah, *Ride in the Whirlwind* (1966), written by Nicholson, and *The Shooting* (1966), written by his good friend Carole Eastman. Though the movies turned out to be too eccentric for distribution in the genre market, they brought considerable attention to all parties involved. Nicholson took them to France in a suitcase "with $400" and "Fred Roos' credit card."[11] He showed them around while becoming conversant with the vibrant *nouvelle vague* film scene.

Within the same general time frame, Nicholson wrote *The Trip* (1967) for Corman. He expected to star as well but was rejected by the ever pragmatic Corman in favor of Peter Fonda, who was much better known. *The Trip* was quite successful but marked Nicholson's last professional association with Roger Corman. His collaboration with Hellman ceased as well. Nicholson moved onto another plane, joining forces with Bob Rafelson and Bert Schneider, known as Raybert. They hung their shingle at Columbia Pictures, headed by Schneider's father and brother. A successful television series called *The Monkees* had provided cash and clout. They made *Head* (1968), directed by Rafelson based on a script cowritten with Nicholson. One year later, they produced *Easy Rider*.

The Art and Craft of Acting

"Jack's career has been achieved by dint of hard work and honing his craft as much as talent,"[12] said Fred Roos, the casting director on *Five Easy Pieces*.

There is mystery at the center of the actor's art, an indefinable *something* we can't quite put our finger on. Actors know it, too. How does a person with his own physiognomy, character, and personality metamorphose into someone else? It's not the beard, wig, or greasepaint, getting fat or thin. Those are mere attributes that assist the transformation—greatly for some actors. Jack Nicholson, for example, is very particular about what his characters wear and sometimes finds the costume himself. For *Easy Rider*, he chose a white suit with suspenders. That garb is from another era, but the dress-up-and-pretend climate of the 1960s made it okay. In *Five Easy Pieces* he wears an old black sweater belonging to Bob Rafelson, his director and close friend—surely not by happenstance.

Why did he make those choices? Nicholson, an exceptionally articulate and conscious actor, could probably tell us, but he rarely divulges his performance secrets. "Don't fall victim to the temptation of revealing your little goodies to your director or your fellow actors,"[13] urged Uta Hagen, the noted actress and teacher, by which she meant the private techniques an actor conjures up to bring his character to life. Constantin Stanislavski, the Russian theoretician, gave students similar advice.

All creative endeavors are mysterious, but the actor's art is uniquely so. Other artists utilize an object external to themselves—a brush and tube of paint, for example, or a pen, pencil, piano, or bow. A painter can step back from his canvas, maybe take a walk or even allow years to pass before the completion of the work—or sometimes paint over what he did and start anew.

An actor cannot do that. The actor is both instrument *and* player. The finest training can do no more than provide an environment for the synthesis—the magical coming together of conscious and unconscious with a fictional creature: the character. All great acting theoreticians say essentially the same thing. Lee Strasberg said the actor brings to his art an instrument already created: himself. His tools are internal: imagination, sensitivity, intelligence. Stella Adler argued that the actor's body *is* his instrument. The most important thing the actor has to work on is his mind.

Sociologist Erving Goffman[14] wrote about the pervasive theatricality of society itself, suggesting that we humans are always playing some sort of "role" and that acting is an extension of the natural order of things. Nicholson would say, "You gotta make it come from the inside. It's all about who you are. That's all you can really contribute. I feel autobiographical about whatever I do."[15]

Mike Nichols, who directed the actor in four very different films over twenty-five years,[16] is exceptionally insightful, not to mention eloquent, about what makes this most fascinating person tick. "Jack is the guy who takes parts others have turned down, might turn down, and explodes them into something nobody could have conceived of… All his brilliance at character and gesture is consumed and made invisible by the expanse of his nature—his generosity, his lovingness, his confidence, his positiveness—and because his nature is so generous, all technical decisions seem to have burned away. It's what makes him the great movie actor he is. You can't see any technique—it just appears to be life."[17]

Ten Iconic Performances

Jack Nicholson is a screen colossus. Because so many different generations have enjoyed his work, a true consensus about what is best or most iconic is daunting.

For the purposes of this book, *Easy Rider* is the line of demarcation. The eighteen features he made prior to the now-legendary road picture that catapulted him to stardom were modestly budgeted genre pictures never broadly distributed. While historically interesting, they can't really compete with the work that followed, when the motion picture world became his oyster. The ten performances spotlighted herein constitute the arc of his career between 1969 and the first decade of the new century.

Easy Rider (1969): His portrait of George Hanson, a do-good Southern lawyer grappling with civil rights issues at a time of crisis in America made Nicholson a star. He received his first Academy Award nomination for the role.

Five Easy Pieces (1970): Bobby Dupea is as different from George Hanson as night is from day. This character study of alienation reflects a perfect meeting of minds between the star and director Bob Rafelson. Nicholson earned a second Academy Award nomination.

Chinatown (1974): The character of Jake Gittes was written especially for Nicholson by his friend and longtime colleague Robert Towne. A noir thriller set beneath the bright Los Angeles sun, it is his only turn as a forties-style fashion plate. He received a fourth Academy Award nomination.

One Flew Over the Cuckoo's Nest (1975): A great American novel was the basis for Nicholson's most emotionally affecting performance as R. P. McMurphy, a man whose unbridled individuality eventually destroys him. For this role, he received his first Academy Award.

The Shining (1980): Nicholson's Jack Torrance stands out as his most terrifying portrait of a man devolving into utter madness. At first denounced, his performance and the film itself are now considered classics.

Batman (1989): A "masterpiece of sinister comic acting,"[18] in the words of *Variety*. The Joker is one of the actor's greatest, most innovative performances.

A Few Good Men (1992): Although in a supporting role, Nicholson dominates the film as reckless Marine officer Colonel Nathan R. Jessep. His performance is especially appreciated by men who've actually been to war. The film is a popular favorite for the line "You can't handle the truth!" He received his tenth Academy Award nomination.

As Good As It Gets (1992): Only Jack Nicholson could be so foulmouthed and get away with it—all the way to an Academy Award, his third.

About Schmidt (2002): A "poignant marker in the career of a major artist,"[19] wrote critic Stanley Kauffmann. Nicholson's portrait of an aging Everyman is both hilarious and deeply touching, and it garnered his twelfth Academy Award nomination.

Something's Gotta Give (2003): Nicholson plays Nicholson in a satire based on his public persona as a committed bachelor. Though only semisweet, the film is his one true romantic comedy, and it's as fresh and surprising as *Easy Rider* was in its day.

Nicholson on the set of James L. Brooks's *Terms of Endearment* (1983).

1

George Hanson

Easy Rider (1969)
Dennis Hopper

"Nik… nik… nik… Indians!"
—George Hanson

It was a sly seduction, a well-considered plan to melt the hearts of filmgoers and simultaneously escape the B-movie trenches in which he'd lingered far too long. The role wouldn't make him a star, but he'd be noticed—remembered. He'd get more work, which was important: he had a family to support.

Jack Nicholson had made eighteen films prior to *Easy Rider* but hadn't been able to break into the mainstream. Although the studios were slowly crumbling, the contract system for employment was still in place and Hollywood's aesthetic of glossy, artificial—even androgynous—beauty prevailed. Tab Hunter was the paradigm. Young Jack, by comparison, was a diamond in the rough—a high-energy cutup with an odd kind of drawl. Interviews and auditions were hard to come by. He had become marginalized, consigned to low-budget genre pictures. It wounded his ego and tarnished his dreamscape.

A much-loved only child, Nicholson had always been a personality kid, someone who stuck out. He had moxie, charm, and a keen, analytical intelligence. Now he meant to use these God-given attributes in the service of a fictional being called "George Hanson."

The character was a doozy—a small-town lawyer in the Deep South who drinks to quell his sorrows and who moonlights for the American Civil Liberties Union. In 1968, are you kidding? When the country was cracking up like no time since the Civil War and members of the ACLU were under siege? But George was no phantom; he existed in black-and-white, placed upon the page by Terry Southern, a sociopolitical satirist whose worldview was similar to George's own.

Nicholson had been cast as George Hanson against the wishes of director Dennis Hopper, who thought he was wrong for the part—too young, too slick. But the film's executive producer, Bert Schneider, disagreed and told Hopper in no uncertain terms to give Jack the part.[20] Shooting was already in progress when the actor paid a visit to the barbershop in Columbia Pictures' basement. The character he was about to play was a straight arrow, not a hippie. Nicholson's scraggly beard had to come off and his hair cut short. He then stopped at Western Costume, a cavernous warehouse stuffed with rentable duds. I'm guessing he didn't know *exactly* what he wanted to wear but permitted the racks and racks of costumes, many with long histories of repeated use, to stimulate his imagination. George Hanson is an attorney… educated… cares about justice… has a good income. His family is prominent, so he mustn't embarrass them. And yet his personal ethos diverges from theirs and that of much of the community. He needs to differentiate himself from their provincialism without making anybody mad.

In a stroke of pure genius, Jack Nicholson made a poetic choice: a white summer suit with trousers held up by suspenders. A pair of dark horn-rimmed glasses completed the look: modern with a touch of retro. White: the symbol of purity and wholeness, of peace. Brides, angels, and doctors wear white, as do the good guys in Western movies. It's the White Knight who saves Alice in *Through the Looking-Glass*. After completing his wardrobe, Nicholson had a handle on George Hanson. He packed his bags and joined the filmmaking troupe in Taos, New Mexico.

The film, of course, is *Easy Rider*, the now-legendary motorcycle movie dreamed up by Peter Fonda and Dennis Hopper. It unspools for quite a while before George Hanson is introduced—lying in a jail cell, wearing the aforementioned rumpled white suit. "Oh, no, what did I do now?" he moans in a molasses-thick accent before staggering remorsefully to his feet. Every moment that follows is fresh and unexpected. Though jailed for drunkenness, George is an elegant man who treats everyone respectfully. He warns the two hippies that their long locks will be like catnip to the local yokels, who might try to shorten them with rusty razor blades. Then he springs them from the hoosegow. Little by little, the audience falls under his spell and is devastated when he is brutally murdered soon thereafter. After the film opened, the *New York Times* declared him "The Man Who Walked Off with *Easy Rider*"[21] in a headline. He accomplished the feat in twenty-five minutes of screen time. He was thirty-two years old.

Jack Nicholson as George Hanson in Dennis Hopper's *Easy Rider* (1969).

A Difficult Start

Ironically, Nicholson had just about given up on an acting career by the time of *Easy Rider*. His screenplays were garnering more attention. *The Trip* (1967), directed by Roger Corman, was exceptionally successful for a "biker" movie. *Flight to Fury* and *Ride in the Whirlwind* were serious pieces, directed by Monte Hellman, in which Nicholson also starred. He costarred with Millie Perkins in *The Shooting* (1966), directed by Hellman from a script by Carole Eastman (a.k.a. Adrien Joyce). While being too offbeat for broad distribution, the films attracted the attention of film cognoscenti in both the US and Europe.

In 1967, Nicholson formed an alliance with Bert Schneider and Bob Rafelson, whose Raybert production company had a huge success with the *Monkees* television series. He cowrote with Rafelson a Monkees movie called *Head*—and then went into *Easy Rider*.

The film had its world premiere at the 1969 Cannes Film Festival. When the audience rose to its feet with a roar, it was crystal clear the film would be a hit and that Jack Nicholson was its heart and soul. "I thought it was some of my best work by far, but it wasn't until the screening at the Cannes Film Festival that I had an inkling of its powerful super-structural effect upon the public. […] I'd been there before, and I understood the audience and its relative amplitudes. […] I thought, 'This is it. I'm back into acting now. I'm a movie star.'"[22] Literally overnight Jack Nicholson had risen from the ashes of a burned-out career—reborn.

The Quintessential American Road Movie

Easy Rider chronicles the cross-country motorcycle trip of Billy (Dennis Hopper) and Wyatt (Peter Fonda), two hippies seeking a life of existential freedom, without entanglement or obligation. Along the way, they interact with a hitchhiker, a farmer and his family, the residents of a commune—and George. Their odyssey is structured as a ballad. Each encounter is a stanza joined to the next stanza by a reprise of ecstatic motorcycle riding through a spectacular landscape. Snippets of songs or musical compositions underline or comment upon each recent experience. It starts with a lucrative drug deal in Los Angeles, after which they head for New Orleans and Mardi Gras.

They meet George Hanson in a Texas jail cell. He's there for drunkenness and they for "parading without a permit"—walking their choppers in the town parade. It's their lucky day because George is a lawyer, scion of a prominent local family. He springs them from jail—then impetuously joins their odyssey.

They camp out in a wooded glade their first night together, sprawl around a fire, and gaze

up at the stars. Offered a marijuana cigarette, George asks, "Lord have mercy, is that what that is?" Soon he is following Wyatt's instructions—puffing the right way and feeling good. When Billy becomes agitated by a strange whizzing object in the sky, George calmly explains that these are UFOs sent by "the Venutians" who "have contacted people at all walks of life," including the government. Even stoned, George seems genuinely convinced that these objects are definitive proof of life elsewhere "within our own solar system"—a positive development. "For once, man will have a godlike control over his destiny; he will have a chance to transcend and to evolve with some equality for all."

The long, moonlit scene, nearly a soliloquy by Nicholson, stops a hairbreadth short of pure camp. It is both hilarious and oddly touching. He delivers the absurd lines with earnest sincerity, in a singsong cadence and with a wacky Southern accent he claims to have modeled after President Lyndon B. Johnson. Years later, cinematographer Lázsló Kovács laughingly recalled how much control Nicholson exercised though high—very high—from smoking countless joints. "It was amazing that he got it word for word."[23] The campfire sequence foreshadows *Easy Rider*'s grander purpose of mirroring the fissures in American society. It also alters the dynamic among the three men. Until then, Billy and Wyatt have secretly felt superior to this "dude" whom

they consider a country bumpkin. Now they see him as more of a cracker-barrel philosopher—not as hip as themselves, of course, but interesting. George is too blissed out to care what they think; he knows who he is, and he is having a helluva good time.

Toward sunset on the next day, they enter Louisiana, in the xenophobic Deep South, with atavistic racial attitudes and practices. Their appearance draws hostile attention from the sheriff and his cronies at a local café where they stop for supper. Insults and epithets are loudly flung about, with one fellow asserting that "they won't make it to the parish line"—i.e., out of the county.

This scene surely presented a challenge to Nicholson, born and raised in New Jersey, far above the Mason–Dixon Line that separates America's North and South. How would the liberal-leaning George react to atrocious behavior by fellow Southerners? Terry Southern would know because he was a Texan. Nicholson portrays George as pained and deeply embarrassed. He refers to their comments as "country witticisms," but he knows the venom is real—dangerous. He says he isn't hungry and suggests they leave—which they do. Afraid of more trouble if they look for a motel, they camp out again that night. Billy and Wyatt are quite unnerved by the experience, whereas George is just plain sad.

George: "Y'know, this used to be a helluva good country. I can't understand what's gone wrong with it."

Billy: [...] "They're scared, man."

George: "Oh, they're not scared of you. They scared of what you represent to them [...] freedom."

Billy: "What the hell's wrong with freedom, man? That's what it's all about."

George: [...] "But talkin' about it and bein' it, that's two different things.[...] Of course, don't ever tell nobody they're not free, 'cause then they're gonna get real busy killin' and maimin' to prove to you that they are..."

And prove it they soon do. All three travelers are asleep when vigilantes stealthily enter their campsite and attack them with baseball bats. George is killed. Billy and Wyatt leave his body where it lies, finally recognizing the peril. They continue the journey until they themselves are murdered, shot with a hunting rifle by two men in a pickup truck.

A Sign of the Times

Easy Rider electrified Americans. The country really was in crisis, and here came a sorrowful film to mirror the discord. People left screenings with their heads lowered, as if from as funeral, many wiping tears from their eyes. Critics quibbled with aspects of the film itself, but all agreed that

Jack Nicholson was astonishing. Vincent Canby's review for the *New York Times* was typical: "Suddenly, however, a strange thing happens. There comes on the scene a very real character [...] a handsome, alcoholic young lawyer of good family and genially bad habits [...] As played by Nicholson, George Hanson is a marvelously realized character [...] Nicholson is so good, in fact, that 'Easy Rider' never quite recovers from his loss..."[24]

Easy Rider defined America's tumultuous 1960s like no other cultural artifact. Why did it resonate so powerfully? Surely there's more to *Easy Rider* than the magic of Jack Nicholson. A bit of context is in order.

A Nation in Turmoil

By the mid–twentieth century, the United States was the most powerful country on earth—an economic behemoth that almost single-handedly lifted up Western Europe after the devastation of World War II. But the country's outward gaze led it to ignore gnawing problems on its own soil—civil rights, for example. Black people began demanding equality through mass demonstrations and marches. People were injured or killed. As the war in Vietnam escalated, antiwar movements sprang up and young men burned their draft cards. "Hell no, we won't go" and "Don't trust anyone over thirty"

were mantras of an entire generation. Eastern religions came into vogue, and drug use.

Personal appearance signified where a person stood on this divide as boldly as a placard. Long hair or a beard could—as in *Easy Rider*—get you killed. Colorful headbands, fringed leather, and tie-dyed cotton garments were *de rigueur* hippie garb. A fashion industry sprang up to reflect the polarities—"flower children" and "revolutionaries" on one side, "straights" on the other.

Unsurprisingly, the crisis extended to the film industry. The studio system was costly and unsustainable. Stars, directors, and producers were unwilling to remain under exclusive contract to a studio. The non-stereotypical young and gifted like Nicholson, Hopper, and Fonda were forced onto the periphery to toil in the fields of cheap, coarse genre films: horror, sci-fi, and biker—the biker movie having largely replaced the Western. Frustration was palpable. *Easy Rider* tapped into these upheavals—societal, cultural, and industrial.

The Impossible Dream

Quite to one side of his iconic performance, Jack Nicholson was instrumental in making *Easy Rider* happen. It was to him that Fonda and Hopper took their twelve-page treatment because of his connection to Raybert Productions. Nicholson immediately liked the idea. "I felt it would be

a successful movie right then. Because of my background with Roger Corman, I knew that my last motorcycle movie had done $6 to $8 million from a budget of half-a-million. I thought the moment for the biker movie had come, especially if the genre was moved one step away from exploitation toward some kind of literary quality."[25]

Nicholson conjured an impossible dream: to have a major studio make a biker flick. He knew Raybert had an ace in the hole. Bert Schneider's father, Abraham, was chairman of the board of Columbia Pictures and his elder brother, Stanley, was president of production. Together with a mere handful of other executives, they controlled the slate of films made at Columbia, a powerful but conservative studio whose most recent Oscar winner was the religious epic *A Man for All Seasons* (1966).

Nicholson boldly made the case for *Easy Rider* to Schneider and Rafelson. Schneider wrote a personal check for $40,000, to cover the cost of one week's shooting in New Orleans at Mardi Gras time, and another for around $350,000— accounts vary—to cover the shooting budget. He became the film's executive producer, and Nicholson would serve as Raybert's liaison to the production.[26] As Bob Dylan sang, the times they were a-changin'.

Despite Schneider's powerful connection to Columbia Pictures, the studio did not agree

to distribute *Easy Rider* until after the screening at Cannes. Once the studio committed, though, the "biker flick" received a first-class marketing campaign. The studio shrewdly forbade any pictorial representation of motorcycles until after the movie opened, using an elegant line drawing of Fonda's face in the ads, below the line, "A man went looking for America. And couldn't find it anywhere…" *Easy Rider* was a phenomenal worldwide success, grossing hundreds of millions of dollars and transforming the American film industry for years to come.

Little Film—Big Legend

Easy Rider made Jack Nicholson a star and became one of the most written-about films ever made. The story of how the "little" film became so big was part of the film's legend and, like most legends, is a mix of truth and fiction. The basic concept supposedly came to Peter Fonda like an epiphany while he was in Toronto on a publicity tour for *The Trip*. Peter telephoned Dennis Hopper, spinning out his dream of an antiestablishment road movie with a social conscience for them to star in and Hopper to direct.

The spark was probably struck earlier—when Fonda and Hopper were sent into the desert by producer Roger Corman to shoot extra footage for *The Trip*. The two men were close, almost like brothers, and relished the experience of doing something on their own, especially Hopper, whose career had stalled.

From this point on, there is wide variance about the project's development, particularly regarding the screenplay's authorship and Nicholson's casting. According to legend, actor Rip Torn was set to play George Hanson but quarreled with Hopper and quit. The role was then offered to Bruce Dern, who said he didn't want to make another motorcycle movie. Nicholson was shoehorned in at the eleventh hour.

But this scenario is "simply not true" according to Terry Southern's biographer, Lee Hill, who interviewed Southern extensively for his biography, *A Grand Guy*. Southern told him that he "wrote the part for Rip Torn, who I thought would be ideal for it […] but he couldn't get out of a stage commitment in a Jimmy Baldwin play. […] So he missed the role of a lifetime." Southern goes on to say that Jack Nicholson "was a good choice because he had that sympathetic quality."[27]

Southern and Torn were both from Texas and close friends. But Torn was literally unable to take the part, and allegations that he walked out or pulled a knife on Hopper just before the onset of shooting were false and harmful to his career. In 1998, Hopper had to pay Torn $475,000 to settle a defamation suit.[28] Hopper finally set the record straight in an interview made not long before his death. "Bert Schneider called me into his office and told me to cast Jack Nicholson,"[29] he states without further embellishment.

In March 2013, Bruce Dern set the record straight with regard to his relationship with *Easy Rider*. "I was never offered the part," he said. "I never read the screenplay or knew anything about the project until Jane Fonda mentioned it during the shooting of *They Shoot Horses, Don't They?* She told me her brother had made a motorcycle movie that was going to be a big hit and that an actor named Jack Nicholson walks off with the picture."[30]

It is incredible that this disinformation has stuck for nearly fifty years. It's not entirely clear why Hopper and Fonda downplayed Terry Southern's role with respect to the development of the concept and actual writing of *Easy Rider*, but the seeds were planted early on. In countless interviews, Hopper has stated that he wrote every word of the screenplay. The full extent of Terry Southern's involvement on *Easy Rider* is detailed in Lee Hill's biography, *A Grand Guy*, and in his British Film Institute monograph on the film.[31]

A Star Is Born

The first rough cut of *Easy Rider* ran more than four hours. Those who saw it say Nicholson's performance stuck out and became ever more impactful as the film was reduced in length. "When I saw *Easy Rider* I thought it was very good, and I asked Dennis and Bert if I could clean up my own performance editorially, which they gracefully allowed me to do," said Nicholson in 1985.[32]

Since George Hanson was conceived and written as an *idea*, as a counterpoint to Billy and Wyatt, he would inevitably take on the attributes and coloration of whoever played him. Had craggy characters like Rip Torn, Bruce Dern or Jack Starrett—names bandied about—played the part, the movie would have felt very different. They would not have provided a sufficient contrast to the ignorant "red neck" murderers. It's unlikely the film would have been so successful with anyone other than Nicholson playing George Hanson. Who possessed his charisma or poeticism? Nicholson's portrayal of George as a different kind of Southern man—decent, sensitive, even sweet—put *Easy Rider* onto a different plane. He gave the film a tragic aura.

The irony is inescapable: in a movie steeped in counterculture idioms, the most conventional character has the greatest impact. In retrospect, it makes sense: George is the only character with whom the average person could identify. Billy and Wyatt, somewhat ludicrous in their hippie garb, are booze-swilling, drug-dealing hippies, smug with Big Ideas, whereas George has a job, family, and roots in the community. "He is not only us—Straightman—by virtue of having a past and a profession, he embodies our relative innocence about drugs even as late as the end of the 1960s," wrote Jeff Greenfield in an appreciation in 1981.[32]

The white linen suit should have been a clue that the fellow in the jail cell wasn't just a "good ole boy"—a humorous put-down term for a working-class Southern man without much couth. The two hippies with him—arrested for "parading without a permit"—know something is up when a guard enters with an aspirin, calling him "Mr. Hanson" and acting like a servant. Billy's survival instinct leads him to strike up a conversation with the genial fellow who, within minutes, has identified himself as a lawyer affiliated with the ACLU. Astounding! "You're lucky I'm here," he chides. "The people hereabouts are trying to beautify America by making everybody look like Yul Brynner". One of his clients had all his hair cut off with a rusty razor blade. Within the hour, "Mr. Hanson" has sprung the hippies from jail, thanked Bob for the aspirin, and graciously allowed

another guard to blackmail him with a veiled threat to inform his father of the arrest. His manners are impeccable.
But what about the white linen suit? Levi's, Stetsons, and cowboy boots are the common modes of dress in a dusty Texas town. Nicholson personally chose his costume, which is redolent of the Deep South. A little research reveals that "Mr. Hanson" is loosely modeled after a recurring figure in novels by William Faulkner, the American writer who won the Nobel Prize for Literature in 1949. A third-generation Mississippian, Faulkner lived in the state his entire life, fighting bigotry with the pen. He introduced Gavin Stevens, a progressive lawyer, in a 1932 short story entitled "Smoke." Such figures were a rarity in the 1930s South, but the Faulkner clan was replete with lawyers, including his great-

grandfather and brother. The character was thought to represent, if not Faulkner himself, certainly his ethos. His decision to live among the very people with whom he so profoundly disagreed took genuine courage. Faulkner was followed by Terry Southern, a multitalented scribbler of satiric novels and screenplays who plucked Gavin Stevens from the writer's pages and reconceived him as George Hanson, believer in "Venutians," extraterrestrial life, bourbon, and justice for all. A Texan by birth, Southern conceived George as more conventional than the two hippies, yet capable of articulating their melancholia about America— "a mouthpiece," Southern called him.[a] Nicholson gives the character poignancy in the careful courtesy he extends to the citizens of his community: respectful but more wary than they realize.

Opposite: Henri Cartier-Bresson's 1947 photograph of American author William Faulkner at his home in Oxford, Mississippi.

Dennis Hopper, Feliciano, Peter Fonda, J. Jefferson and Jack Nicholson at the Cannes Film Festival in 1969.

The counterculture movement was statistically marginal to American life, despite its high profile. Had there not been a character with whom the average person could identify, *Easy Rider* wouldn't have racked up those huge box office grosses. Hopper and Fonda were glamorized versions of hippies shown on television and in newspapers—fellows who scandalized their families by being arrested for sit-ins or drug use. Most people wouldn't be so foolish. But George Hanson was something else again—a good-hearted soul. In identifying with George, audiences could taste the exotic world of the counterculture scene without getting dirtied by it.

Jack Nicholson was a star waiting to happen. *Easy Rider* got him.

2

Robert "Bobby" Eroica Dupea

Five Easy Pieces (1970)
Bob Rafelson

"If a person has no love for himself, no respect for himself, no love of his friends, family, work, something—how can he ask for love in return? I mean, why should he ask for it?"
—Catherine Van Oost, Bobby's lover and his brother's fiancée

Five Easy Pieces arrived with fanfare, premiering on opening night at the New York Film Festival in 1970, the year after *Easy Rider* took the world by storm. A buzz was in the air. The film-hip audience knew it came from the same Hollywood contrarians who'd made the stunning road picture, and they were eager to trip out again—with Jack Nicholson.

Waves of adulation had continued to wash over Nicholson for his portrait of a do-good country lawyer in *Easy Rider*. It sometimes felt as if the whole world had fallen in love with "Jack," as he soon would be called, with his sweet nature and casual charisma. They assumed those same qualities would be present in future roles.

But a very different Jack treads through every scene of *Five Easy Pieces*—a sullen, angry, tortured soul who drifts from place to place in search of an "auspicious beginning." He's an oil rigger when the movie opens, a prodigal son in the middle, and exits at the end as a hitchhiker en route to nowhere. Bobby Dupea's identity is ever-fluid; he doesn't know who he is, only who he isn't. Nicholson plays him true. He never pulls his punches, makes excuses, or pleads for understanding and compassion as actors often do when playing despicable characters. The character is not admirable or likable, yet, as incarnated by Jack Nicholson, he's riveting. In 2003, critic Roger Ebert remembered that premiere: "the explosive laughter, the deep silences, the stunned attention […], and then the ovation. We'd had a revelation. This was the direction American movies should take: Into idiosyncratic characters, into dialogue with an ear for the vulgar and the literate, into a plot free to surprise us about the characters, into an existential ending not required to be happy."[34]

Nicholson's performance is what keeps us vitally interested in the film itself. We feel Bobby's pain and see the fix he's in but haven't a clue what caused the turmoil until the film reaches the halfway point. Its unorthodox narrative structure makes it puzzling, hard to follow, and elusive. But it does, eventually, get under the skin—and throb.

In hindsight, it's clear that *Five Easy Pieces* predicted more accurately than *Easy Rider* Nicholson's career to come. In future decades, he would startle his public with portraits of repugnant men—in *Carnal Knowledge* (1971), *The Shining* (1980), *The Postman Always Rings Twice* (1981), and many others—including a racist homophobe in *As Good As It Gets* (1997), for which he won a third Academy Award. But on that evening, September 10, 1970, festivalgoers were in a bit of shock, slowly realizing that Jack Nicholson is not predictable—not a Hollywood charm-boy but a highly complex individual willing to take risks that challenge and shake up an audience. It was a corrective as stinging as a slap in the face. Bitter herbs instead of a milk shake.

Nicholson and Rafelson would ultimately make five films together between 1970 and 1997, though none was as successful as *Five Easy Pieces*, which was amply honored with four Academy Award nominations—for best picture, screenplay, actor, and supporting actress (Karen Black). The New York Film Critics Circle named it best film of that year while honoring Jack Nicholson, Karen Black, and Bob Rafelson. Rafelson also won the Directors Guild of America award as best director of 1970. It remains one of the most fascinating films from the "Golden Era" of the 1970s.

Inspirations

It cannot be said that *Five Easy Pieces* is a near-sequel or sibling to *Easy Rider*, though it has often been described as such. *Pieces* springs from entirely different sensibilities, predominantly those of director Bob Rafelson, who cowrote the story, and screenwriter Carole Eastman—each of them a stubborn iconoclast. Bobby Dupea's curt, take-me-as-I-am personality incorporates aspects of both individuals, and the character's peregrinations are strikingly similar to Rafelson's early life.

Born in New York City, into a middle-class Jewish family, Rafelson ran away from home at age fourteen because it was "stultifying" and he "didn't want to do the family thing." It's tempting

Nicholson as Bobby Dupea in Bob Rafelson's *Five Easy Pieces* (1970).

to regard *Pieces* as at least semiautobiographical. Rafelson says "only vaguely," recalling being affected by the early death of people close to him. "It was an era of self-destruction, wandering, searching,"[35] he said in 2012.

But *Five Easy Pieces* was written in 1969, and its genesis was two prose treatments Rafelson wrote "about a wandering young man."[36] He turned these over to Carole Eastman when they began discussing a possible film for their mutual friend, Jack. Rafelson also gave Eastman a magazine article about Ted Kennedy that attributed his self-destructive behavior at that time to the pressures of being the youngest son in a wealthy and powerful family. The piece obviously struck a chord with Rafelson.

Carole Eastman's background was entirely different from Rafelson's, which made their similarities all the more surprising. She was an Anglo–Angeleno whose family were craftsmen in the film industry who mingled with Russian immigrants and other Europeans with deep affinities for music. Her father had also worked in the oil fields dotting Southern California.

Eastman and Nicholson had been close friends for at least a decade—since attending an acting class together in the late 1950s. She wrote *The Shooting*, the 1966 Western directed by Monte Hellman in which Nicholson stars with Millie Perkins and Warren Oates. His character, a gunman named Billy Spear, has a lot in common with Bobby Dupea, notably a tough-mindedness verging on sociopathy.

Nicholson plays tough-minded characters exceptionally well, possibly because he shares their need to draw a protective circle around themselves. He's said to be more than able to hold his own with regard to contracts, compensation, and encroachments upon himself. "I've never allowed anybody to think they could own me,"[37] he said in 1985. Eastman knew her friend well.

It often feels as if Nicholson, as Bobby, is channeling Rafelson, a sometimes curt individual who felt no compulsion to charm—as opposed to Jack, who often did. In a 1985 interview, the actor said of his relationship with Rafelson: "It falls into the realm of the exceptional. We are real close. Since we started off writing together, we know each other very well."[38] Prior to *Pieces*, they had cowritten a script for *Head*, improvising "under the influence of Timothy Leary's little white pills."[39] The experience brought about an exchange of intimacies, and they developed a shorthand way of communicating with each other. It's not improbable that Nicholson absorbed, almost by osmosis, aspects of the director's hurtful, bewildering childhood.

Nicholson's approach to his character is merciless—perhaps more so than needed. He is an actor who can charm the birds from the trees if he so chooses, yet he does nothing whatsoever to make Bobby Dupea likable, forgivable,

The Road as Metaphor for Life

A "road movie" is filmspeak for "travel with consequences." One or more characters embark upon a journey, stopping along the way to see someone or have an experience, which alters their life or perspective. It is a quintessentially American genre, a representation of the country's size and expansion through movement. It owes something to Henry Ford, inventor of the Model T, who compelled the government to build a network of roads in order to sell his cars. Road movies are as diverse as the byways upon which their stories unfold, and in form they can be a quest, an escape, or a search for love, redemption, or self-definition. The character(s) must always have a powerful need to leave behind the familiar for the mystery and promise of the unknown or, as in Homer's eighth century BC epic poem *The Odyssey*, struggle to get back home. Change is implicit.

Five Easy Pieces is not a definitive road picture because Bobby Dupea (Jack Nicholson) does not—apparently—change. But "the road" does serve as a powerful metaphor of his frantic search for a place for himself in the world, an identity. It's part of his backstory, his peregrinations before the movie begins, as well as his unknowable future when it's over. It's also an actual route Bobby drives by car to visit his dying father: California Highway 1, which runs alongside the Pacific Ocean between Mexico and Canada.

Jack Nicholson has made five road pictures,[b] the most famous being *Easy Rider* (1969), in which he portrays a small-town lawyer named George Hanson. But *Easy Rider* wasn't George's trip. He is merely a stop along the way—an experience—for the two protagonists, played by Peter Fonda and Dennis Hopper. His magnified presence on *their* trip is due to the tragic manner of his demise—and to Nicholson's performance. Awareness of the road movie as a distinct genre blossomed after *Easy Rider*. Studios hoped to replicate its success with low-budget films such as *Two Lane Blacktop* (1971), *Vanishing Point* (1971), *Electra Glide in Blue* (1973), *Alice Doesn't Live Here Anymore* (1974), *Bring Me the Head of Alfredo Garcia* (1974), *W.W. and the Dixie Dancekings* (1975), and *Smokey and the Bandit* (1977). The invention of new lightweight camera equipment facilitated the process, though no film to date has ever had the impact—or box office success—of *Easy Rider*.

or even comprehensible—except in the last scene with his father. Something about this particular character's dilemma must have struck a nerve with Nicholson. His portrait of Bobby Dupea is the most low-key and artless of all his touted performances.

It is my belief that Bobby Dupea—both as written and as performed—was hugely influenced by the actor's personal relationships with Bob Rafelson and Carole Eastman. Rafelson is skeptical but does point out that "'directed by' provides a pipeline going in two directions."[40] Indeed, Nicholson made more than forty films after *Five Easy Pieces*, but his portrait of Bobby is unique in several aspects: its emotional content, felt truth, and absolute refusal to entertain.

Flight Forward

Five Easy Pieces opens in an oil field, where Bobby works as a rigger. Nicholson did enough research to know what riggers do and is believable as a workingman spewing profanities just like the others. His robotic movements and sour expression suggest something other than a Zen-like state of oneness with the job, but we think nothing of it—yet.

What's surprising is his inability to stick up for himself with the woman he lives with, Rayette (Karen Black). A baby-doll type with a whispery voice, Rayette covets a career as a country singer and plays that type of music nonstop. It drives Bobby bonkers, but he can't explain why or, worse, put his foot down.

Our first real clue that the guy isn't who he seems is when he and a coworker get stuck in traffic. Bobby impulsively gets out of the car, acts the fool, then jumps aboard a truck transporting a piano—and starts playing. The music merges with the cacophony of the road, making the level of his proficiency uncertain, but he looks like he knows what he's doing and stays at the piano as the truck veers off in another direction. Nicholson studied piano for some time before starting the film.

Two back-to-back events elicit Bobby's startling capacity for ruthlessness—when he learns Rayette is pregnant and when he learns his father is dying. Marriage and parenthood are traps he means to avoid, and we see it in Nicholson's icy, determined face. A short time later, he quits his job.

We next see a man transformed—nicely dressed, with a pleasant expression—driving into Los Angeles to see his sister, Partita, a pianist, who's there to make a recording. They are affectionate with each other, but when she mentions their father's deteriorating medical condition, he says, "Don't tell me about this." She persists, and he finally agrees to come for a visit—"one week at the most," and he'll maybe go on from there into Canada.

Even in his mind, Bobby is ever in motion—always heading out to some other place, or thinking about it. The psychiatric term for this dilemma is "flight forward"—a compulsion to escape the unbearable present. Bobby is also trying to figure out a way to escape Rayette.

Five Easy Pieces is quite elliptical in this section, possibly because some of the scenes weren't scripted. Eastman and Rafelson would eventually do battle over the amount of improvisation Rafelson allowed as well as the scenes he cut or changed. Eastman removed her own name from the credits, instead using her *nom de plume*, "Adrien Joyce."

An Antiromantic Film

One of the most fascinating and hard-to-play aspects of *Pieces* is Bobby's ambivalence toward Rayette. She has little formal education and works as a waitress. He pretends to be a blue-collar worker when he's actually from a wealthy, cultured family. He treats her contemptuously—but stays. It's never clear why they are drawn to each other, though she is quite beautiful.

Rayette is an infuriating presence, confident enough in her beauty and sexiness to get her way irrespective of how it affects the other person. Karen Black is brilliant in her creation of a certain type of faux-helpless, manipulative female whom women detest and men accept with a degree of amusement.

One night in a motel bed, Bobby withdraws, turning his back and pulling the coverlet up to his despairing eyes. But Rayette won't accept this. She wants to make love, and she won't stop until Bobby fulfills her need. "Guess I'll have to count the sheep… one, two, three, four, five, six, seven," she teases in her Marilyn Monroe–ish voice. "Look at this old cold shoulder. What *am* I going to do about it?" He finally turns over resignedly, saying, "You know, if you wouldn't open your mouth, everything would be just fine." To call *Five Easy Pieces* merely "antiromantic" would be to understate its scabrous depiction of male–female relations—with regard to all of the characters, not just Bobby and Rayette.

The scene in which Bobby packs to go see his family is exceptionally powerful. Rayette wants to come with him, but he says no and storms out with his suitcase. But once inside the car, he is incapable of turning the key in the ignition and actually leaving. We don't know, at this point, that he was never allowed self-determination while growing up, but we do see his utter paralysis. He can't do it, he cannot leave Rayette behind, and so he has a tantrum—beating the steering wheel and crying out in real anguish. His volition returns only when he decides to get her. In a 2009 interview, Rafelson said he did only one take of the car scene. "Jack understands rage because he has it in his own life."[41]

Bobby, Rayette, and two lesbian hitchhikers (Helena Kallianiotes and Toni Basil) stop at a diner. Bobby orders a chicken salad sandwich, hold the chicken. "I want you to hold it between your knees," he sneers at their irritable waitress (Lorna Thayer).

Opposite, top: On the ferry to the Dupeas' house on an island in Washington state.

Opposite, bottom: Bobby offends his brother, Carl, by claiming to have worked as a Las Vegas musical review rehearsal pianist.

Two Distinct Worlds

An unspoken truce prevails as Bobby and Rayette drive north toward Washington. She sings the corny country songs he hates; he keeps his eyes on the road. They pick up a couple of hitchhiking lesbians and stop for lunch. Bobby tries to order an omelet with tomatoes and toast, though the menu says no substitutions, and has a nasty back-and-forth with the waitress. The scene ends when he sweeps the dishes off the table.

Audiences love this silly scene, which has nothing to do with the rest of the movie. "It could be lifted and never be missed,"[42] observes Rafelson. The director blames himself for its inclusion, because a similar scene was in one of the treatments he provided Eastman. She gave it her own spin, though, providing cameos for Helena Kallianiotes and Toni Basil, old friends of Nicholson's, Rafelson's, as well as hers.

At the midpoint of *Five Easy Pieces*, the locale changes from the rough-and-tumble working-class part of Southern California to the Edenic island where Bobby grew up, which is reachable only by ferry. The bifurcation is savagely wrought, pitting the blue-collar world against that of the affluent and cultivated, as if never the twain shall meet—which they don't, not in this movie.

You Can't Go Home Again

Bobby Dupea is the son of a revered musician who raised his children in a musical hothouse and moved them to an isolated island to minimize distractions. Bobby was expected to become a concert pianist but turned his back on the profession and left home at an early age. He is deeply scarred by being bent to his father's will, never allowed to make his own choices, train for another line of work, or develop his own identity. This is where we find him at the beginning of the film: in such a state of abject confusion that he might never discover his natural self.

After Bobby and Rayette arrive in Washington, *Five Easy Pieces* feels like a different movie— except for Bobby, whose anger quotient edges ever higher. He abandons Rayette in a motel and makes the trek to the capacious Dupea residence. He hears piano music as he approaches the front door—and smiles. Except for that fleeting moment, Nicholson plays Bobby's arrival at his former home stone-faced and without a trace of visible emotion. He looks around… but not too much. We get the feeling little has changed. Certainly he hasn't changed in his feelings toward "home."

He walks in the direction of the music, opening the door. Inside are a man and woman playing facing pianos, so absorbed they don't

even notice him. These are his brother, Carl (Ralph Waite), and Carl's fiancée, Catherine (Susan Anspach). Bobby closes the door without making his presence known. What kind of homecoming is this? His family members surely knew his arrival was imminent. He could be the prodigal son were there a loving family to greet him. Bobby seems to have anticipated this reaction, though.

Nicholson chooses to play all of the early scenes involving his family as highly suppressed—outwardly showing very little, assuming the audience will make its own connection to the homily "You can't go home again."

He eventually comes upon Partita, who is combing their father's hair. She smiles warmly and turns the wheelchair around, so father and son can see each other. There is no sign of recognition from the father, who has had a stroke. "He doesn't even know who the hell I am," Bobby sighs. Whatever marginal fantasy he may have allowed himself about this encounter evaporates like a puff of smoke. He realizes he is irrelevant. *Irrelevant.* It didn't matter whether he returned or not. A kind of *déjà vu* of despair sweeps over him, which festers over the coming days as he becomes increasingly erratic.

We learn a lot about Bobby at dinner that night. His brother's fiancée, Catherine, asks the questions we would ask if we were at the table. How long have you been away? What have you been doing? It turns out the family didn't know where Bobby was for a long time. A detective was considered but never hired. Carl doesn't recall how many years have passed since he saw his brother—or perhaps he only underestimates to be cruel.

Bobby seduces Catherine in retaliation, at least in part, as well as to have an excuse to stick around a while. After all, he has nowhere to go—nowhere that he *wants* to go. The scene of Catherine's condemnation, when she tosses him to the wolves, as it were, is excruciating. He neither loves nor respects himself, she says, and therefore has no right to ask for love from others. Nicholson again suppresses any visible emotion, saying simply "okay" when she is finished explaining why she will stay on the island with Carl.

To Cry or Not to Cry?

The tension in the house explodes after Rayette arrives unexpectedly, having run out of money at the motel. Here is where Nicholson has an opportunity to really display his range, writhing with shame at Rayette's ignorance while simultaneously despising those who look down on her. His attraction to simpler, less well-educated people like Rayette becomes easier to understand.

Just before leaving, Bobby wheels his father to a promontory overlooking the bay and makes an attempt to communicate—a painful, awkward scene. "I don't know if you'd be interested in hearing about me," Bobby begins, going on to say that he knows his father wouldn't approve of his lifestyle: he moves around a lot, always looking for "auspicious beginnings."

"I'm trying to imagine your half of this conversation," he continues. "My feeling is, I don't know, that, uh, if you could talk, we wouldn't be talking; that's pretty much how it got to be before I left. Are you all right? I don't know what to say. […] The best that I can do is apologize. We both know that I was never that good at it anyway. I'm sorry it didn't work out."

Both Rafelson and Nicholson have spoken of this scene being contentious because of the issue of emotion: to cry or not to cry. Rafelson said he must cry; Nicholson didn't want to. "I told Jack we had to see the underbelly of this character; he had emotion but it was all bottled up—blocked."[43] In 2013, Rafelson remembers the conflict: "I kept him up for two days—not easy when you're shooting on a low budget. We took a full day off, Saturday. We had been close friends for a long time. Jack had been emotional with me many times. He felt it was unfair for me to take advantage of our personal relationship. I responded by saying it would be unfair if I did not."[44]

On the morning of the shoot, Nicholson took a pencil and started crossing out the lines in the script, writing something else. Rafelson says, "I told him I didn't care what words he spoke; I only wanted the emotion. I cleared the set, locked the camera, operated the mike on a long boom, sat his father just off camera." While the camera was rolling, Rafelson turned away and hid behind a piece of equipment so Nicholson couldn't see him. After a long silence, Rafelson finally spoke: "Jack, are you done?" Nicholson was furious because his director hadn't even watched the scene! Rafelson says he has never looked at that scene. "I know what it cost the actor to perform. Many believe Jack changed the course of acting in that moment, demanding that actors reveal the truth of themselves."[45]

In 1986, Nicholson told a journalist that the crisis between him and Rafelson produced one of his finest moments as an actor. The scene lived powerfully in his memory: "I can see the grass on the hill and I know what the air was like and I can remember that day and what happened after we went on."[46]

An Uncertain Ending

On the road again, presumably back to Los Angeles, Bobby and Rayette stop for gas. She enters a convenience store to purchase candy;

Awkwardness ensues when Rayette comes to dinner. (Middle, from left to right: Ralph Waite, William Challee, John P. Ryan, Lois Smith, Karen Black, and Jack Nicholson.)

Following pages: Bobby and Catherine (Susan Anspach) hold up traffic at the ferry to talk about their affair.

Bobby and Rayette ride back to the mainland.

Opposite: A final act of "flight forward" — Bobby abandons Rayette at a gas station and hitchhikes north.

he goes to the men's room. This, too, is a potent scene. Bobby removes his coat and gazes into the mirror, penetratingly, for a long time. Is he asking, "Who is that person?" There is definitely some kind of meaningful exchange between himself and his mirror image—or an *attempted* exchange. As in the family scenes, Nicholson's face is drained of feeling, showing almost nothing.

When he exits the men's room he discovers a huge log truck has rolled up while he was inside, blocking his view of Rayette and his car. He speaks to the driver, then jumps into the passenger seat of the truck. As he shivers, the driver asks if he has a jacket, because it's going to be cold where they're heading. Bobby mutters something about everything being lost when "everything in the car got the shit burned out of it" but "I'm fine... I'm fine." The truck pulls out, going in the direction from which Bobby just came—due north, possibly to Canada. Who knows?

There is then a long shot of Rayette at the gas station, looking for Bobby. Rafelson never puts the camera closer lest her dilemma defuse the effect he is seeking—the flight of Bobby Dupea. "The end of the movie is the way people felt about the end of the decade—the 1960s," said Toby Carr Rafelson, production and costume designer for the film. "Hope is gone. What will replace it? What will happen to Bobby Dupea?"[47]

Eastman's original ending had the two characters being killed in an auto accident. "Together, we changed the ending," Rafelson explains, "because I did not want character to die at the end. It would be too easy. Rather he be doomed to wander..."[48]

3

J. J. "Jake" Gittes

Chinatown (1974)
Roman Polanski

"Forget it, Jake. It's Chinatown."
—Lawrence Walsh, Jake's assistant

The closing lines of *Chinatown* resonate with all the menace and ambiguity that has brought us to that moment. Yes, the last few scenes are set in that section of Los Angeles, but those five words are less geographical than they are a metaphor for mystery, intrigue, and corruption. The gravity given them invokes a sense of biblical apocalypse, like Sodom and Gomorrah, echoing as something best forgotten, quickly and without looking back, lest we, too, turn into a pillar of salt.

Jack Nicholson had become both a critically revered performer and a bankable movie star by the time *Chinatown* came out in 1974. He had notched up three Academy Award nominations and been named best actor at the Cannes Film Festival the previous year for *The Last Detail* (1973, adapted by Robert Towne from Darryl Ponicsan's novel). Had there been any lingering doubt about his standing, *Chinatown* would soon put a cork in that discussion.

Set in 1937 Los Angeles, the neo-noir mystery centers on J. J. Gittes (Jack Nicholson), a private detective with a bottomless caseload of errant husbands and wives. The pay beats what he used to make as a cop in the district attorney's office, providing a nice office and assistants. But the cases are so predictable he has become enveloped by ennui. Jake Gittes has seen it all—or so he thinks.

Nicholson doesn't have a lot of snap, crackle, and pop in the early scenes. It's disconcerting to find the actor so sedate and low-key, but it's obviously by design. Also by design is his appearance—high-fashion outfits, color coordinated right down to the two-tone shoes; hair parted in the middle and slicked back with pomade. It's a new look for Nicholson, but the viewer must get used to it: *Chinatown* is styled in the manner of a 1940s studio picture and exudes glamour from start to finish.

When a woman introducing herself as Evelyn Mulwray (Diane Ladd) appears in Gittes's office one morning, intuition tells him what she wants to know: whether her husband, Hollis Mulwray (Darrell Zwerling), is having an affair. Only the man's prominence as chief engineer of the Water Department gives the job fillip, and Gittes actually tries to dissuade her from the pursuit—to no avail.

A contract is drawn up, and Gittes begins by tailing the older man to an apartment building. The photo he snaps of Mulwray and a teenage girl in a "compromising position" winds up on the front page of the tabloids. Job done.

But the following day a different woman (Faye Dunaway) shows up saying *she* is Evelyn Mulwray. She is accompanied by her lawyer, who is threatening to sue Gittes. Every twist and turn of screenwriter Robert Towne's labyrinthine saga stems from that opening salvo.

Until Faye Dunaway as the real Evelyn Mulwray appears, Gittes has seemed supremely confident. But the two Evelyns have stuck a pin in his balloon, and he must deftly shift gears. He doesn't like being set up. Who did it? Why? With a new respect for mystery, and new resolve, Gittes has to become a real gumshoe instead of collecting easy money for the painfully obvious. As his armor is removed, he becomes emotionally vulnerable.

Gittes's segue from jaded investigator to potential victim showcases Nicholson's remarkable ability to externalize a character's inner life by infinitesimal degrees. In his first scene with Dunaway, he transitions seamlessly from braggadocio to surprise to uncertainty; he portrays cockiness, boredom, confusion, and a genuine work ethic within the opening fifteen minutes. This is a very different persona from the hard-boiled types of yore, who are always on top of every new development.

Sam Spade, Philip Marlowe, and J. J. Gittes

The private eye—or gumshoe, shamus, tail, dick, sleuth—became a staple of popular fiction in the 1930s. The stories of writers like Dashiell Hammett and Raymond Chandler adapted easily to cinema, with *The Thin Man* series (starting in 1934), *The Maltese Falcon* (1941), and *The Big Sleep* (1946) being among the most popular and enduring. The next generation of sleuths rarely made it to the big screen, migrating instead to television. The private eye as a movie protagonist was just about absent for two decades.

Chinatown's ultra-complicated narrative makes it akin to *The Big Sleep*, directed by Howard Hawks and starring Humphrey Bogart, but their protagonists are quite different. "[...]

Nicholson as Jake Gittes in Roman Polanski's *Chinatown* (1974).

49

Opposite: Confronted with a real mystery, Gittes struggles to solve the case.

When the real Evelyn Mulwray (Faye Dunaway) shows up, Gittes is thrown for a loop.

Gittes is the opposite of [Philip] Marlowe: the tarnished knight [of *The Big Sleep*] who wouldn't do divorce work, who didn't care about his physical appearance," says Towne. "Where Gittes was more than something of a dandy, a clotheshorse, absolutely vain, and Jack playing him that way was half-kidding. [...] He's cynical, but with his own kind of idealistic streak."[49]

Roman Polanski invokes the classics—more Sophocles, less Chandler. As critic Mark Graves writes: "Gittes is a muckraker, earning his living by taking pictures of people engaged in extramarital affairs to support his clients' divorce cases. By engaging in such low-brow activities in order to elevate his personal appearance to high-class, Gittes has shattered the wall of morality that usually separates the private-eye from the world he must investigate," which "[...] foreshadows Gittes' inability to fulfill the role of the ingenious private investigator when a real issue arises, because he is not distanced enough from the outside world to appropriately observe or change it. [...] [H]e is always trying to fit new clues and information into predetermined categories."[50]

It's something of a stretch for Nicholson to play dumb unless the character is essentially a cartoon, as in *The Fortune* (1975), *Man Trouble* (1992), and, most notably, *Prizzi's Honor* (1985). In *Prizzi*, the actor had to change his voice and manner of speaking to be credible as a cretinous

hit man—either that or wear a bad wig per director John Huston, who forbade him to depict the character as intelligent.[51] He pulled it off and got his eighth Oscar nod. But his portrait of J. J. Gittes doesn't have a similar built-in signal. Part of what makes *Chinatown* confusing is having a razor-sharp actor play a near-clueless character. The film is fast approaching its denouement before we fully realize that Gittes is in over his head, a naïf thrust into a conspiracy and a shocking family psychodrama. The fancy duds belie the actuality: that he's like a tumbleweed caught in harsh desert winds.

Polanski's decision to tell the yarn from the private eye's perspective, by shooting from behind Gittes or over his shoulder, adds to the difficulty of simply following the storyline. When Gittes is knocked unconscious, for example, the screen goes black, returning to focus as he regains his senses. So Gittes and the viewer, perforce, discover the twists and reversals of *Chinatown* simultaneously. We, like him, assume Mulwray is having an affair with the girl in the picture; we likewise assume the broken glasses in the koi pond are his. Like Gittes, we skitter ahead of, or lag behind, the story.

The director explains that he read Chandler and Hammett when he was a young man He loved them and always looked forward to adapting them. The movies of their work, he thought, were wonderful but they often missed

Opposite, top: Nicholson with producer Robert Evans.

Opposite, bottom: Polanksi, Nicholson, and other members of the cast and crew on set.

In a cameo role, Polanksi himself slices Nicholson's nose.

Following pages: Gittes seems to get more lost at every turn.

the main element—the first person. In all of the books, the story is told by the detective. This, he says, is why he shot *Chinatown* from Gittes' point of view, over his shoulder. "I cheated sometimes a little bit [...], but the viewer is not aware of it."[52] *Chinatown* also departs from the older film noirs by taking place under the bright sunlight of Los Angeles.

Making a Conspiracy

Originally titled *Water and Power*, *Chinatown* was meant to be part of a trilogy Towne and Nicholson would do together.[53] Longtime friends, they had met in the late 1950s in an acting class, where they began dreaming and scheming about how to find success in the film industry. A native of Southern California, Towne is passionate about its history. The germ of an idea crossed his mind in 1969, while he was killing time between rewrites of *The Last Detail*. He stumbled across an article called "Raymond Chandler's L.A." in *West* magazine. The stunning photos used as illustrations looked like 1930s Los Angeles though they had just been taken. "I began to realize and reflect upon how much had been lost about the city in the intervening 30–35 years. [...] I went to Jack and said 'What if I wrote a detective story set in L.A. of the '30s?' He said 'Great.'"[54] That was part one of the script's development.

Part two evolved in Oregon, where Towne was perched temporarily, playing a small part in *Drive, He Said*, Nicholson's directorial debut film. "I hadn't really read Raymond Chandler at that point, so I started reading Chandler." He also found a book, *Southern California Country: An Island on the Land*,[55] which discussed shenanigans underlying the development of Los Angeles from a desert filled with orange groves to a modern metropolis—specifically an incident in 1905 when oligarchs created an artificial drought in order to drive farmers off their land, which they then purchased for pennies. "And I thought 'Why not do a picture about a crime that's right out in front of everybody. Instead of a jewel-encrusted falcon, make it something as prevalent as water faucets, and make a conspiracy out of that.'"[56]

The fledgling screenplay got momentum when Robert Evans, Paramount's production chief, approached Towne about adapting *The Great Gatsby*. Towne turned him down but persuaded Evans to underwrite the new project. By the time the script was finished, Evans had become an independent producer at Paramount. He thought Towne's script plus Nicholson plus Roman Polanski would be a fine send-off for his new career. Evans knew Polanski, having worked with him on *Rosemary's Baby* (1968). He hoped the director's darkly ironic sensibility, combined with his own penchant

"Down these mean streets
a man must go who is not
himself mean, who is
neither tarnished nor afraid.
The detective must be
a complete man and a
common man and yet an
unusual man. He must be,
to use a rather weathered
phrase, a man of honor.
He talks as the man of his
age talks, that is, with
rude wit, a lively sense
of the grotesque, a disgust
for sham, and a contempt
for pettiness."
—Raymond Chandler,
The Atlantic Monthly,
November 1945

There were detectives in the
silent era, but the gumshoe
didn't come into his own
until the talkies. Given
voice, he fell into one of two
categories—the debonair,
exemplified by William
Powell, or the working stiff.
Chinatown's Jake Gittes
is somewhere in between
the two poles. His striking
sartorial elegance aspires
to Powell's Nick Charles
(*The Thin Man*). However,
without the fancy duds and
manicures, he's closer to
cinema's most beloved stiff,
Humphrey Bogart—though
he's not a carbon copy.
Scriptwriter Robert Towne
aspired to bring "a character
who was a little bit different"[c]
to the genre, and one critic
thought he succeeded:
"Nicholson wears an air of
comic, lazy, very vulnerable
sophistication that is this
film's major contribution
to the genre," opined
Vincent Canby.[d]
Gittes was custom-made
for Nicholson by Towne, who
thought that "his kind of
insouciance suggested itself
for a very cocksure detective
who was cynical but with
a hidden idealistic streak,"[e]
who really thought he knew
all the answers but in
fact had no notion how evil
somebody could be.
The 1930s and '40s were
the upper-crust P.I.'s heyday.

Stars like Powell, Ronald
Colman (*Bulldog
Drummond*, 1929), and
Walter Pidgeon (*Nick Carter,
Master Detective*, 1939)
presented the detective as a
matinee idol—witty, urbane,
and fashionably dressed,
dazzling the eye in black-
and-white.
The 1941 *Maltese Falcon*—
its third incarnation—
established the "hard-boiled"
school, a distinctly American
subgenre with a stress on
action, not complex puzzle-
solving or witty repartee
as favored by the British.
The tough-minded detective,
like Dashiell Hammett's
Sam Spade, emerged from
battles over union organizing
in Western states. Coming
later, Raymond Chandler's
Philip Marlowe was a more
romantic figure—a modern
knight who operated on
an elevated moral ground.
Bogart's playing of both Sam
Spade (*The Maltese Falcon*)
and Philip Marlowe (*The
Big Sleep*, 1946) was so
definitive that he virtually
reinvented the gumshoe
persona for decades to
come. While tipping his hat
to Bogart, Nicholson regards
his character as "a different
guy altogether. He's a nosy
pragmatist, a snoop."[f]

for visually stunning movies, could result in something special. He turned out to be correct on all counts.

A Nosy Fellow

The *Chinatown* envisioned by Towne and Evans demanded a "movie star" performance—the kind of studied, well-coiffed and manicured "Am I not the cat's meow?" look we associate with Tyrone Power or Robert Taylor. The stellar production design team of Richard Sylbert and his sister-in-law Anthea was hired—he for set design and she for costumes. The city of Los Angeles itself supplied everything else.

Nicholson had never played a true leading man, and he wanted to—badly. He believed his offbeat looks had prevented an earlier career breakthrough and now, with the wind behind his back, joked about showing off his "perfect tear drop nostrils,"[57] according to Towne. The opening scenes in particular do indeed present him as a glamour-puss, like stars of the 1940s—shot from the most flattering angles, with beautiful lighting and lingering images of his near-perfect profile. The custom-made suits of cream and ivory with matching shoes and fedora seem a bit extravagant for a private investigator, but, hey, this film is directed by Roman Polanski, about whom the late critic Andrew Sarris wrote, "His talent is as undeniable

as his intentions are dubious."[58] We need to prepare for just about anything.

And "just about anything" happened a few weeks into the shoot. Polanski had already incurred Robert Towne's wrath by overhauling his screenplay, and now he decided to spoil his star's leading man fantasy. Though it wasn't in the script, Polanski made a spur-of-the-moment decision to mar Gittes's face with an injury. And he would make the cut himself, in a cameo role as a thug. The scene takes place at night, near a reservoir. The diminutive director steps out of mist and shadows to slit Gittes's nose—fake blood spurting everywhere. It's a shocking act that adds an element of danger, but Nicholson had to wear a big white bandage in the middle of his face for most of the picture. In an 2006 interview, Polanski could barely suppress a smile when he remembered how frightened the actor was. "It—the knife—added drama to Jack's expression."[59] Nicholson does indeed look frightened as well as in pain.

Faye Dunaway recalls the actor's distress in her autobiography, *Looking for Gatsby*. "A few days into the film, Roman decided he wanted to cut Jake's nose. He liked the metaphor of a nosy private detective getting his nose slashed. [...] The special-effects man created a knife with a hinged tip that would give with the least amount of pressure, with a tube of blood hidden on one side of it. But there was always the fear that somehow that hinge would catch, and you can

Humphrey Bogart in Howard Hawks's *The Big Sleep* (1946).

Evelyn Mulwray hires Jake to investigate her husband's death, but fails to mention she's the daughter of Noah Cross.

Following pages: Gittes confronts Noah Cross (John Huston), but comes up short.

see it in Jack's eyes, despite the fact he checked the knife in Roman's hand before every take to make sure he was holding it right."[60]

Nicholson has never spoken of the matter in a public forum, but can we not assume he was disappointed? Certainly, Dunaway believed that's how he felt. The incident may have contributed to Nicholson's eventual realization that he was a character actor, not a traditional romantic leading man; if so, the bandage was a blessing in disguise. Certainly, it is memorable.

A Naïve Gumshoe

Jake Gittes and Evelyn Mulwray come to terms after she learns the truth—that someone pretending to be her hired the detective to follow her husband. She agrees to drop her lawsuit. Gittes, however, is too stoked with curiosity to stop sleuthing. He may not know exactly what the hell is going on, but something's amiss. By happenstance he is present when Hollis Mulwray's body is pulled from the water—drowned, according to the coroner. Gittes suspects murder and contracts with Mrs. Mulwray for $5,000 to find out how he died. Water issues, he figures, are a key to the subterranean goings-on. Various clues lead him to Noah Cross (John Huston), former owner of the Water Department. Gittes learns that Cross was the late Hollis Mulwray's business partner as well as being Evelyn's father.

Against her wishes, Gittes accepts Cross's luncheon invitation. Gittes is like a lamb to the slaughter, totally out of his league with the crafty and ruthless power broker. Cross has his way with Gittes, asking questions with faux jocularity. Gittes answers every single one, unaware the "lunch" is really an inquisition, and he's revealing information crucial to the implementation of Cross's evil plans.

It is an extremely fascinating scene, in part because Nicholson was so well acquainted with Huston as the father of Anjelica, his girlfriend at the time. Huston is a powerful personality in his own right. He got away with addressing Gittes as "Mr. Gitts"—an error of pronunciation that irritated Jack, according to Dunaway. Nicholson plays the scene with his eyes cast downward toward his plate, like an errant child confronted by an intimidating father. It's impossible to know whether he made that choice because Gittes is intimidated by Cross or because John Huston was sitting across the table. Either way, it works.

Even after Gittes has put all the pieces together—a conspiracy to divert water from the San Fernando Valley to Los Angeles was masterminded by Cross, who murdered Mulwray—he runs afoul of a parallel mystery that is too deep for mere detective work. Having been primed by Noah Cross to believe Evelyn hates the teenage girl he photographed with Hollis Mulwray, Gittes follows her. Peeking through the

window of a house she enters, he sees Evelyn with the girl. What he glimpses seems to confirm, as per Cross, that the girl may be in danger. Instead of barging into the house, however, he lies in wait for Evelyn in her car. Later, he confronts her and slaps her several times as an incentive to talk.

Finally the awful truth comes tumbling out. The girl is actually Evelyn's daughter, sired by her father, Noah Cross, which means she's also Evelyn's half sister. Her late husband was not having an affair with the child; to the contrary, he was helping care for her—to keep her out of Noah Cross's clutches. Cross wants custody of the girl. Nicholson's reaction to these stunning revelations is essentially a non-reaction. He has made a similar choice in other films where the scene is certain to stun or debilitate the viewer. He might assume that the content itself has sufficient impact, that a reaction from him of shock or disgust is not only unnecessary but would ruin the moment.

The last fifteen minutes of *Chinatown* are a frenzied mishmash of scenes that would seem like the bumblings of Inspector Clouseau if the situation weren't so tragic. While trying to escape with her daughter, Evelyn is shot to death by the police. Noah Cross grabs the girl. Gittes realizes he caused this twin tragedy by allowing himself to be used by Cross, and by never really understanding what was going on. He is devastated. His assistants lead him away, Walsh saying, "Forget it, Jake. It's Chinatown."

Denouement

Towne and Polanski quarreled bitterly over the ending. In Towne's version, Evelyn shoots her father and manages an escape with the child. Polanski opposed such an ending. "If you are telling a story of corruption, of evil, you have to show the result of evil. That's how the tragedies of Greek theater were conceived."[61] Taking his cue from Sophocles, Polanski reconceived Towne's original ending. Shortly before he shot the scene, he gave his notes to Nicholson, requesting that he write the dialogue. Thus Polanski made Nicholson an accomplice, allowing the two of them to carry out the theme of *Chinatown*: that men with power feel free to have their way. In time, Towne forgave Polanski, and today he says the director was right. Of *Chinatown*'s eleven Academy Award nominations, the only winner was Robert Towne.

Nicholson's performance throughout the film is surprisingly straightforward—no winks or histrionics, scant evidence of his usual charm, and little to no vulgarity. The character loses his cool only once, in a barbershop, when a fellow customer disrespects his profession. Nicholson plays it as genuine, almost righteous anger. "I make an honest living," he says. The *New York Times* critic Vincent Canby wrote that Nicholson "wears an air of comic, lazy, very

vulnerable sophistication that is this film's major contribution to the genre."[62]

Costume designer Anthea Sylbert, who also created Nicholson's costumes for *Carnal Knowledge* and *The Fortune*, declared him "the easiest to dress—not from the way he's built—but because he is extremely open and free about trying anything."[63]

Faye Dunaway praised Nicholson extravagantly in her autobiography, *Looking for Gatsby*. "I could never have asked for a dearer friend to me or more loving person than Jack. […] There are few people that I have loved working with as much as Jack. He was just a dreamboat, a real gent. He's smart, he's an intellectual, he's articulate. […] As an actor, he's there in the moment and there's always humor running through his work […]. [H]e's a true American original."[64]

Polanski and Nicholson remain great friends. "Jack is the easiest person to work with that I have come across in my whole career," says the director. "First of all, he's tremendously professional, and secondly, it's very easy for him to do anything you ask. I think he spoils the director, and the writer, because any lines you give him sound right, even if they're awkward or badly written. When he says something, it sounds authentic. He never asks you to change anything."[65]

4

Randle Patrick McMurphy

One Flew Over the Cuckoo's Nest (1975)
Miloš Forman

Dr. Spivey: "Do you think there is anything wrong with your mind, really?"
McMurphy: "Not a thing, Doc. I'm a goddamn marvel of modern science."

R. P. McMurphy is among the most potent fictional characters ever put upon a page—feisty and devious like Scarlett O'Hara, primitively male like Stanley Kowalski. As the antihero of Ken Kesey's legendary 1962 novel, he was already burned into the reading public's imagination long before a film adaptation came along. The producers knew they needed someone exceptional to play McMurphy—a gifted actor, yes, but also a riveting and charismatic personality the audience would care about until the tragic denouement. They considered men as disparate as Marlon Brando, Burt Reynolds, and Gene Hackman before concluding that only one man really fit the bill: Jack Nicholson.

At a high point in his career, Nicholson had already received an astonishing four Academy Award nominations within five years—for *Easy Rider*, *Five Easy Pieces*, *The Last Detail*, and *Chinatown*. The rascally Navy signalman he played in *Detail* was akin enough to McMurphy to suggest the reservoir of energy, willfulness, and humor he could bring to the character.

But Nicholson's suitability for the role went well beyond his star status. Unlike urban, "ethnic" actors such as Al Pacino, Robert De Niro, or Dustin Hoffman, Nicholson's hazel eyes and fair complexion marked him as someone of Anglo–Irish descent, as any fellow called "McMurphy" is likely to be. Nicholson also has plenty of swagger and verve, enduring traits of Irish–American men found, for example, in the plays of Eugene O'Neill and the novels of Jack Kerouac. *On the Road*'s Dean Moriarty is a virtual re-creation of Neal Cassady, the wild-man poet of the traveling clan, and both incarnations (real and fictional) are said to have inspired Kesey in creating McMurphy. The brawling Irishman—often poetic, just as often tragic—is an iconic figure with deep roots in American history, culture, and literature. Nicholson fits him to a tee. His knack for wringing laughter from unlikely scenarios was an added plus for a story taking place in a mental institution.

Although generally thought of as a comedy, and marketed as such, *One Flew Over the*

Cuckoo's Nest is actually a harrowing depiction of institutional power, of the myriad legal ways institutions subdue and crush the human spirit. The enduring success of both novel and film testify to the universality of Kesey's thesis. On the book's fiftieth anniversary in 2011, literary critic James Wolcott wrote: "*Cuckoo's Nest* conveys the wonder of a fable with the force of a fist. […] It seems more (curse the word) *relevant* than ever, the oppressive forces it mutinied against having only gotten more immersive and influential in our lives since McMurphy got zapped."[66]

The story begins as McMurphy arrives at the mental institution from a prison farm where he has been incarcerated for statutory rape. The movie never explains why he decided a "cuckoo's nest" or "loony bin" would be a better spot to serve out his sentence, only that he behaves incorrigibly until his wish for a transfer is granted. "No sacrificial lamb has ever worn a better wolf disguise,"[67] says Wolcott.

A Sixties Icon

It was my good fortune to spend a week on the set of *Cuckoo's Nest* in the spring of 1975 for a journalistic assignment. I watched in amazement as the crew applauded Jack Nicholson's takes again and again—the rarest of honors. It was obvious to everyone that a remarkable, spookily personal performance was unfolding before their eyes. Nicholson himself knew he was in the zone. Sometimes he reached such a Zen-like state of oneness with his character that the director's voice calling "Cut!" caught him unawares and he'd blink in surprise. He appeared to be pleased by the applause but also embarrassed, as if it were *his* soul being exposed instead of a fictional character's. And perhaps it was, poetically speaking, since transformative acting always emanates from the actor's inner self.

With the exception of a few exteriors, the film was made at the Oregon State Hospital, a facility for the mentally ill in Salem, Oregon. The set and production offices were part of an entire ward made available to the producers. This meant that the filmmaking unit—director, producers, cast, and crew—spent its entire working day *within* the hospital, among patients deemed sufficiently advanced to play extras or work on the crew.

Nicholson as R. P. McMurphy in Miloš Forman's *One Flew Over the Cuckoo's Nest* (1975).

65

McMurphy loves to get a rise out of the hospital staff (Mimi Sarkisian and Nathan George).

Opposite: Nicholson on set with producer Michael Douglas (right) and his brother Joel (middle), the film's unit production manager.

The blurring of "reel" with "real" was further enhanced when the resident psychiatrist, Dr. Dean R. Brooks, agreed to play the movie's Dr. Spivey.

I was struck by the gravitas of the filmmakers and crew despite the hilarity played out in front of the camera. It was unsettling to work within a mental hospital, especially one where electroshock therapy and prefrontal lobotomies—procedures central to the story—had been performed. Dr. Brooks constantly reassured everyone they were a relic of the past. However, their cinematic enactment was expected to be so disturbing it was placed at the end of the shooting schedule, long after my departure. Months later, when I saw the finished film, I was grateful because those scenes are among the most disturbing in modern cinema.

Kesey's personal experiences provided the springboard for the novel. In 1959, while a graduate student at Stanford University, he volunteered for a CIA-financed study of psychoactive drugs at Menlo Park Veterans Hospital in Northern California. He later worked there as a night aide, continuing to use hallucinogenic drugs such as mescaline and LSD. "It gave me a different perspective on the people in the mental hospital […]," he explained much later. "But psychedelics are only keys to worlds that are already there. […] Drugs don't create characters or stories any more than pencils do."[68] He became close to the patients and didn't like what he saw—the catastrophic brain surgeries,

drugs, and other methods used to control and manipulate them. Kesey believed the patients were merely "different," not "insane," and he wrote the novel quickly, in a state of incendiary rage and despair. As a budding novelist, he naturally wanted to create a work of literary merit, but his most passionate wish was to change attitudes toward mental illness and its treatment. He succeeded in both respects beyond anything he could have imagined.

The novel flew into legend on the wings of the antiauthoritarian 1960s zeitgeist. It became a bestseller and, by 1965, a Broadway hit starring Kirk Douglas. Douglas optioned the screen rights but couldn't cut through studio resistance to such "dark" material. When he became too old to play McMurphy, he turned the project over to his son, Michael Douglas. Bypassing Hollywood, Michael instead approached Saul Zaentz, owner of Fantasy Records, a respected jazz label in Berkeley, California. Zaentz agreed to finance the film.

The new partners hired Miloš Forman[69] to direct. A prominent figure of the Czech New Wave, Forman lived in exile in New York, having fled Czechoslovakia after the 1968 Soviet invasion. His Czech films—*Black Peter* (1964), *Loves of a Blonde* (1965), *The Firemen's Ball* (1967)—were sociopolitical satires and his one American film, *Taking Off* (1971), a comedic variation. Forman's personal history—his family had perished in the Holocaust—as well as his

directorial sensibility more than qualified him to adapt a story whose overarching theme is the citizen versus the state.

Before beginning the film, Forman lived for an extended period at the Oregon State Hospital, where the film would be shot. "I had to do it to clear my head," he said. "When I agreed to direct the film, I was flooded with psychiatric magazines from well-meaning friends. Finally, I refused them all because the more I looked into it, the more confused I became. One of the challenges [...] is that you are describing mentally ill people at a time when doctors don't know what mental illness really is. I resolved just to concentrate on the story of a man, and to see with my own eyes the behavior of the patients. I was practically living with them, and I can tell you how they walk and how they talk, but I do not know what kind of disease they have. I can only define 'mental illness' as an incapacity to adjust within normal measure to ever-changing, unspoken rules. If you are incapable of making these constant changes, you are called by your environment crazy. Which of course indicates that mental illness is a social disease. And that's what the book is about: it's a metaphor of society."[70]

Nicholson, too, relocated to Oregon well in advance of filming, renting an apartment near the hospital. He mingled with patients and staff, using his observations for extensive improvisational sessions with the other actors. "For more than four months, I spent the days there and would come out only at night [...]. I'd have dinner in bed and go to sleep and then get up the next morning—still in the dark—and go back to the maximum security ward. It was basically being an inmate, with dinner privileges out."[71] This was not his first exposure to mental illness. "I had worked in a veterans' hospital a few years before, assisting a woman who was teaching an acting class to advanced schizophrenics [...]. Also a girl that I went with, her father had a nervous breakdown, and I had to put him through the charity wards of mental institutions in Los Angeles [...]."[72]

The Star as Outsider

The inmates and hospital staff were played by actors who were unknown at the time, but the producers and director believed a star should play McMurphy—"somebody from the world known to us entering a world unknown,"[73] in Forman's words. Even today, mental illness is the most mysterious and terrifying of all human conditions. A star rivets the audience on the character, compelling viewers to experience the story through them.

Finding an actress to play Nurse Ratched, the supervisor of McMurphy's ward, was unexpectedly difficult. The character, by size and import, is a major role anyone might covet. However, feminism was becoming a socio-political force and several high-profile stars, Angela Lansbury and Anne Bancroft among them, declined to play such a despicable figure. Louise Fletcher, a little-known but intrepid actress, leaped into the void to play the part and snared an Oscar for her steely, break-the-mold performance. Jack Nicholson was the film's only familiar face.

The screenplay is structured as a battle of wills between McMurphy and Nurse Ratched. Their struggle for dominance begins the moment he enters the hospital. As soon as the handcuffs are removed, he bounces into the ward like a rambunctious kid onto a playground. "Goddamn, boy, you're about as big as a mountain," he exclaims to Chief Bromden (Will Sampson), a tall, taciturn Indian. When told the Chief is deaf and dumb, McMurphy does a little war dance. Though decidedly irreverent, his whoops bring smiles to the faces of men starved for diversion. The power of laughter cannot be underestimated as a technique for winning hearts and minds.

The opening scene between newcomer and patients exemplifies the astuteness of star casting. McMurphy's behavior is outrageous and would be seriously off-putting if a lovable actor already known for his mischievous spirit weren't playing the part. McMurphy turns away from the nonresponsive Chief to the patients' card game. He horns in, circling around the table making quips about each man's hand, interrupting their train of thought by flashing dirty pictures from his own deck, and contriving a scheme to "win" their cigarettes.

Nicholson uses clownery very effectively, playing the scenes broadly, employing his trademark grin and derisive laugh to keep everyone on eggshells. He turns McMurphy into a whirling dervish of hyperactivity—ringmaster of all he surveys—and is, of course, highly entertaining. That's McMurphy's implicit trade-off: I will make you laugh and you will do my bidding. He's clever, insidiously so, but he doesn't realize that every move he makes is observed by Nurse Ratched.

On the conceptual level, Nicholson needed to make a dramatic contrast between his character's off-the-street liveliness and the flattened effect of the drug-addled patients. He also had to start high in order to calibrate McMurphy's gradual disintegration within the institution.

The War Begins

The first joust between McMurphy and the nurse happens at "Medication Time." He objects to taking the "horse pills" being handed out. "I don't want anyone to try and slip me some saltpeter, y'know what I mean?" She threatens to give him the "medicine" by other means, at which point he makes an elaborate show of swallowing the capsule. But when her back is turned, he spits it out with such force it strikes a patient, Harding (William Redfield), in the

forehead. Harding warns that she might've seen him. "Woo! Woo!" he responds. "God Almighty, she's got you guys comin' or goin'." The DVD version omits a later scene in which Nurse Ratched spots the large orange pill, picks it up off the floor, and places it in McMurphy's outstretched hand, making it his first defeat.

McMurphy's interview with Dr. Spivey evolved from extensive improvisations between Nicholson and Dr. Dean R. Brooks, the hospital's game psychiatrist. The shooting script has thirty-seven pages of printed takes, most with minor variations, before a "script" of sorts was settled upon and the scene took its final shape. The playfully devilish Nicholson was clearly trying to shock the doctor with comments too obscene to ever reach the screen.

This is one of the sequences I watched being filmed. Every take was hilarious. Nicholson—adept at playing overlapping actions within a scene—presents McMurphy as both impudent and clueless. He enters the doctor's office as if he were an equal, there for a chat, and immediately creates a diversion by commenting on a desk photo of the doctor with a large fish. Dr. Brooks—as Dr. Spivey—holds his own very well, having undoubtedly seen all manner of con men in his day. Ignoring McMurphy's attempts to ingratiate himself, he gets right to the point: why did prison authorities think him mentally ill? "I fight and fuck too much,

I guess," McMurphy responds laconically, as if it weren't important. But when the doctor brings up the statutory rape charge, McMurphy exhibits a darker side. Almost snarling, he rises from his chair and leans across the doctor's desk, describing the girl's genitals in vivid, boldly coarse language. She was so enticing, he says, that he couldn't resist, and he doubts the doctor could've either had he been in McMurphy's place. It is an almost shocking act of defiance, heightened by Nicholson's in-your-face delivery. Few stars are as willing as Nicholson to be that crude on-screen.

Rabble-rouser

The first third of the film revolves around McMurphy's desire to watch the upcoming World Series and serves to escalate his tug-of-war with Nurse Ratched. He tantalizes the patients with a fantasy of exiting the institution to see a game at a downtown bar. He promises to create an escape route by smashing a window with a huge control panel attached to the floor of the tub room. "We're gonna go out through the hall, downtown, sit down at a bar, wet our whistles, and watch the ballgame."

As Nicholson plays the scene, it's impossible to know if McMurphy actually believes he can do it—it's probably beside the point. His goal is to ingratiate himself with the patients, and he

An imaginary baseball game. Left to right: Sefelt (William Duell), Fredrickson (Vincent Schiavelli), Scanlon (Delos V. Smith Jr.), McMurphy, and Martini (Danny DeVito).

Opposite: Page 154 of the manuscript of Ken Kesey's *One Flew Over the Cuckoo's Nest*.

Following pages: McMurphy argues with Harding (William Redfield) as the others look on.

makes a herculean effort, almost collapsing in the process. "Well, I tried, didn't I, goddammit? At least I did that," he says, and they agree. They know he is a scoundrel but admire his nerviness, wishing some of it would rub off on them. But they also know the dangers of departing from the drill—of defying the staff. Though they are benumbed by fear and tranquilizers, we can almost read their minds as they guardedly observe McMurphy's game. Is this guy a comedian, a bully, a "plant," or a hyperaggressive male soon to be taken down by "the Combine"—Chief Bromden's apt term in the book for the nexus of legal, societal, and institutional forces at play? They've seen assertive men undone by electroshock therapy and lobotomies. The patients are hipper than McMurphy, but he doesn't know it—not yet. This scene also foreshadows the movie's fantasy ending, in which Chief Bromden does pull the piece out. He escapes through the broken window, becoming the "one who flew over the cuckoo's nest" of the title.

Something the film does well without belaboring it is to show how much apprehension the staff feels around the patients. The antidepressants forced upon them like sacred wafers are as much to minimize their fear as to help the patients. As a recidivist criminal with experience facing law enforcement, McMurphy is keenly aware of their fear and tries to manipulate it for his own purposes.

As the Series continues, the possibility of seeing a game pops up again. By now, McMurphy has learned he must approach Nurse Ratched cautiously and politely asks if the television can be turned on so he and the other men can watch the Series. She says okay, if the majority of them wish it, and asks him to take a vote. She knows he can't come up with the right numbers because so many of the patients are "vegetables." She's being unfair and everyone knows it; however, the other patients have long ago ceded their autonomy to her.

Not McMurphy. As furious as a bull charging toward a red cape, he decides to create a "pretend" World Series. The patients watch the blank screen, and he announces the plays with gusto. This scene, too, was improvised, and the lines below are from the shooting script, not what's actually spoken in the film.
McMurphy: "He's into his wind-up. Here's the pitch… It's a hit! It's a hit!"
Cheswick: "It's a hit! It's a hit!"
Martini (jumping up and down): "I saw thum! I saw thum!"
Scanlon: "Me, too! Me, too!"
Harding: "Yes, I see it! I see it!"
McMurphy (on his feet): "Ya-hoo, let's play ball!"

Nicholson, a big sports fan, gives his absolute all in the scene, driving the patients into a frenzy with his outsize energy and enthusiasm. Nurse Ratched panics and shuts down the game. McMurphy is summoned to Dr. Spivey's office once again.

Every once in a while, but not often, there comes a performance so bitterly truthful, incandescent, and bracingly real that it feels like an incarnation. Jack Nicholson achieved that rare synthesis as R. P. McMurphy, the antihero of *One Flew Over the Cuckoo's Nest*. How did it happen? The performance has the mood, specificity, and sense of danger found in sketches by Goya or paintings by Thomas Eakins. As a portrait, it is multilayered. Bits and pieces of three decades emerge, beginning with the 1950s, when the actor was in high school. "Cool was everything," he recalls. "You never let on what bothered you. Pegged pants, pleats, the thinnest tie, shoulders, one button in front"[g] was de rigueur dance garb. By age seventeen, he was in Los Angeles, confronting the specter of "twenty-five people walking around L.A. in red jackets who looked exactly like James Dean. But Marlon is my idol…"[h]

In 1957, *On the Road* was published and had a sensational impact. Dubbed "the Bible" of the Beat Generation, it introduced a mesmerizing figure called Dean Moriarty, who was based on Neal Cassady, hero of the novel's itinerant cross-country travelers. Cassady's poeticism and sexual magnetism made him a muse to a string of writers, starting with Jack Kerouac. A graduate student at Stanford University when he read *On the Road*, Ken Kesey found the rootless, spontaneous lifestyle it depicted deeply appealing. He left school and started hanging out with West Coast Beats; he volunteered for a clinical trial on hallucinogenic drugs at a local mental hospital—then worked there as a night aide. He witnessed the power of institutions to destroy nonconforming men. Anguished, he set his first novel in a similar institution, with R. P. McMurphy as a character who breaks rules like Cassady but also cares about others like Kesey himself. *One Flew Over the Cuckoo's Nest* was published in 1962.

Jack Nicholson and Ken Kesey were born two years apart. Kerouac and Cassady were older, but they, too, reflected a generation of American men who couldn't abide fences.

By the miraculous process of creative osmosis, Jack Nicholson's portrayal of McMurphy combines Cassady's wild spirit with Kesey's sense of moral outrage. It is an indelible screen performance that many consider to be his greatest.

Kesey   154

(Chapter)

There's long spells —three days, years—when you can't see a thing, know where you are only by the speaker sounding overhead like a bell buoy clanging in the fog. When I can see, the guys are usually moving around as unconcerned as though they didn't notice so much as a mist in the air. I believe the fog affects their memory some way it doesn't effect mine.

Even McMurphy doesn't seem to know he's been fogged in. If he does, he makes sure not to let on that he's bothered by it. He's making sure none of the staff sees him bothered by anything; he knows that there's no better way in the world to aggravate somebody who's trying to make it hard for you than by acting like you're not bothered.

He keeps up his high-class manners around the nurses and the black boys in spite of anything they might say to him, in spite of every trick they pull to get him to lose his temper. A couple of times some stupid rule gets him mad, but he just makes himself act more polite and mannerly than ever till he begins to see how funny the whole thing is—the rules, the disapproving looks they use to enforce the rules, the ways of talking to you like you're nothing but a three year-old—and when he sees how funny it is he goes to laughing and this aggravates them no end. He's safe as long as he can laugh, he thinks, and it works pretty fair. Just once he loses

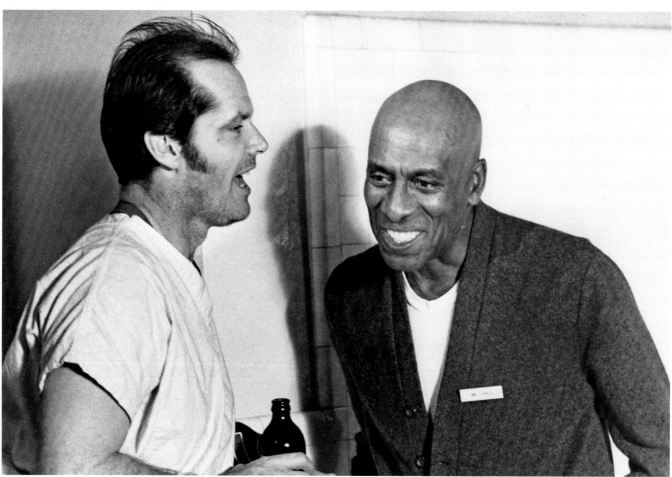

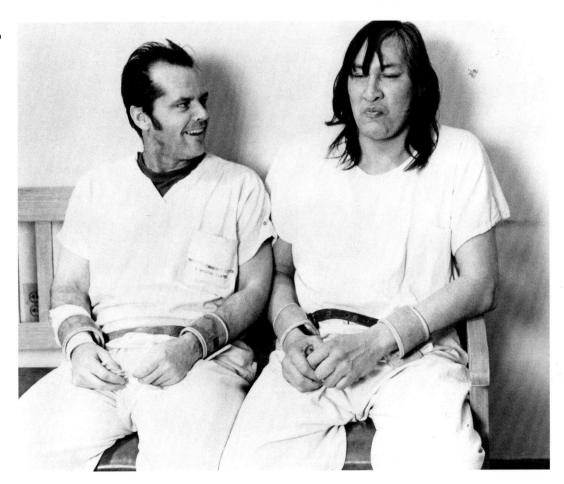

An Unsucessful Seduction

This time, other professionals are included to observe the by-now-notorious troublemaker, R. P. McMurphy. He fulfills their expectation, calling Nurse Ratched a "cunt" because "she likes a rigged game." He says her power plays make you "want to kill." Nicholson does not pull his punches: he displays in myriad moments just how diabolical this character is, and follows through soon after with an attempt to actually kill her.

Nicholson doesn't soften the character's misogyny; if anything, he heightens it by his body language and facial expressions. The demonizing of Nurse Ratched was controversial even when the book was published. The book and screenplay blame Nurse Ratched, not Dr. Spivey, for the lobotomy to which McMurphy is ultimately subjected. Nicholson takes considerable care to underline this all-important dynamic and told a reporter that he made the character's supreme confidence in his sex appeal part of his "hidden" strategy. "[T]his guy's a scamp who knows he's irresistible to women and expects Nurse Ratched to be seduced by him. This is his tragic flaw. I discussed this with Louise [...] only with her. That's what I felt was actually happening with that character—it was one long, unsuccessful seduction which the guy was so pathologically sure of."[74]

One of the film's most powerful scenes comes when McMurphy is made aware of his actual legal situation. When he contrived a transfer from the prison farm, he figured he could leave the institution after serving his original sentence. That assumption is almost certainly why he was so reckless. However, there is no set release date for a mentally ill person. He can't leave until the psychiatrists say he's fit. He learns this from Washington (Nathan George), a staff member, while swimming and then brings it up in the group therapy session that follows. McMurphy's realization of how he has entrapped himself is played by Nicholson with subtlety and true Stanislavskian truth—from the inside—his face filled with self-recrimination and defeat. McMurphy knows he has alienated the hospital staff and cannot expect a favor. Despite this new knowledge, he continues to infuriate those with power over him. He is incapable of altering his behavior, even to save himself.

But he does change focus. From this point forward, McMurphy's antics are oriented to benefit the patients at least as much as himself—to lift them out of their dronelike state. His ideas about this are wholly misguided and, in fact, dangerous. A boating trip he illicitly arranges does bring joy to the patients, but they barely avoid a catastrophic accident. A second—and final—stunt he pulls ends disastrously, however, and leads to his undoing. He arranges for a midnight party with prostitutes and pushes the stuttering, virginal Billy (Brad Dourif) into a room with one of them. Afterward, when

Opposite, from right to left:
Sampson, Forman, Josip Elic
("Bancini"), and Nicholson
on the basketball court.

McMurphy fights with
Washington (Nathan George)
after Cheswick's explosion
over cigarettes.

Nurse Ratched threatens to tell his mother, Billy kills himself. It is this incident that the hospital staff uses to justify performing a prefrontal lobotomy on McMurphy, destroying his brain function.

Different, Not Crazy

R. P. McMurphy is a complex, multilayered character, an unholy mix of good and bad, and extremely difficult to play. Nicholson's performance is an honest one. Even in the earliest scenes, he projects the character's dark side and never tries to make excuses for him. Within the gestalt of Ken Kesey's concept, the character represents preternatural freedom, including sexual, even when it conflicts with law and tradition. Kesey designed the character to be manipulative, exploitive, and dishonest but not deserving of destruction. The novel rages against pressures to conform.

Forman's directorial style greatly enhances Nicholson's performance. Hollywood directors of that era were expected to keep the camera on the star, but Forman's shots incorporate other characters along with McMurphy. He uses close-ups sparingly and gives each character his "moment."[75] By the end, we know the other patients as well as we do McMurphy, and share their pain when he is destroyed.

Jack Nicholson is a powerful actor with an outsize personality. Had Forman placed his image front and center throughout the film, the performance might have lost its potency, become tedious. It is to Nicholson's credit that he embraced Forman's visual design for the film. Many stars would not accept visual parity with supporting players. Nicholson bowed to the primacy of his director.

In interviews with the press after the film was released, Nicholson admitted that "It was unnerving, shooting in an actual mental institution. I got depressed at first because it was hard to comprehend that you can't talk to someone. I've had to reason with people who are eccentric but when someone has killed people… or just sat in the closet and counted his shirts for a month, you don't feel like you're on a one-to-one basis."[76] There is no clearer evidence of the impact of the environment than his performance itself, which stands out as the most raw and emotional of Nicholson's entire career.

In 1976, *One Flew Over the Cuckoo's Nest* won all five major Academy Awards—best picture, actor, actress, director, and screenplay—and there were many other honors and accolades. The film was hugely successful and had a profound impact within the mental health community. It exposed the devastating effects of electroshock therapy and prefrontal lobotomies, which theretofore had been a "dirty secret" among professionals. It questioned the validity of ambiguous psychiatric diagnoses as well as institutionalization as a treatment modality. By the end of the 1960s, these procedures were largely phased out. Kesey's wish to do good came true.

5

Jack Torrance

The Shining (1980)
Stanley Kubrick

"Once I begin to work on a particular movie, I consider myself to be the tool of the director."
—Jack Nicholson, 1985[77]

The Shining created an uproar when it was released, and it remains Jack Nicholson's most controversial film. Director Stanley Kubrick and his two costars, including Shelley Duvall, came under scathing attack by many critics as well as Stephen King, whose best-selling novel provided the basis for the film. The naysayers claimed it was overblown, unclear, and insufficiently frightening— it didn't play by the rules of the horror genre. The film was not remembered at awards' time and did not do well at the box office.

Today, *The Shining* is widely considered to be a masterpiece of meditative horror—one of the scariest movies ever made. It is a retrospective favorite, especially at Halloween, when it is sometimes shown in cemeteries to ensure everyone gets a double dose of fright. The still photo of Nicholson's maniacal face, framed by the ragged hole in a door, is reproduced more often than any other image from his sixty-eight films, and his satanic cackle "Heeere's Johnny!" is gleefully imitated by moviegoers who weren't even born when the film first came out.

In terms of Nicholson's career arc, *The Shining* signaled an artistic and possibly personal change of direction that lasted more than fifteen years. Up until then, he had been considered a naturalistic actor, albeit with an edge. After *The Shining*, he incorporated surrealism into his performances, veering toward a "Grand Guignol" style—shocking, audacious, gory, and often angry beneath the surface. *Prizzi's Honor*, *The Witches of Eastwick*, *Batman*, and *Wolf*, in addition to *The Shining*, are stellar examples of his work from this period.

Bold, risky, nonnaturalistic acting is rarely found on the "Big Silver," as Nicholson calls the movie screen. Most actors can't pull it off or are afraid to try, especially stars who don't want to muddle their image or look foolish. But Nicholson has always taken risks. His adventurous spirit is what drew Kubrick to him for *The Shining*, along with his keen intelligence. "He brings to a role the one unactable quality— great intelligence."[78]

Hell Is Other People

It's not uncommon for a novelist to disagree with a film adaptor, but the gulf between Stephen King and Stanley Kubrick was profound. King wrote of a blocked writer whose wife and son get the brunt of his frustration, especially when he is inebriated. The story had roots in King's own life and held great meaning for him. He set it in a castlelike hotel haunted by an evil force that afflicts his protagonist and incites him to do bad things. The character is eventually redeemed.

King strongly opposed the casting of Jack Nicholson. He felt the actor was identified in the public mind with McMurphy in *One Flew Over the Cuckoo's Nest* and could not be credibly "redeemed"—a view some might find naïve. He may also have suspected Kubrick of being disdainful toward the character. Otherwise, why cast Nicholson, a lethal satirist of the male prerogative? In this respect, he was not entirely off base. Kubrick had no use for the supernatural except as a device. He believed evil to be an inherent human attribute and holds Jack Torrance responsible for his actions. There is no redemption.

The two men also had wildly differing views of marriage. To King it was a refuge whereas Kubrick viewed the institution an existentialist hell where each partner dutifully plays a "role" inimical to the other. The huge, isolated hotel was no different from the room in Jean-Paul Sartre's *No Exit*—a space without doors or windows, from which there is no escape. King's fictional wife is strong and resilient; Kubrick's a pitiful enabler, barely able to summon the gumption to save her son and self—though it is significant that she finally does so. "Hell is other people," Sartre famously said. In Stanley Kubrick's version of *The Shining* each family member is an "other."

Kubrick had wanted to try his hand at a horror film for years but couldn't find suitable material. He liked King's novel because it provided a framework for certain ideas he wanted to explore about family dynamics. According to novelist Diane Johnson, who adapted the novel with Kubrick, "It was the atmosphere of growing fear within the domestic circle—the underlying hate between father and child, and child and father" that intrigued him. "What interested him most, however, was *why* this situation was horrifying.

Nicholson as Jack Torrance
in Stanley Kubrick's
The Shining (1980).

There was something very basic here… an archetypal situation that was more interesting than the business about the ghosts."[79]

Johnson acknowledges that she and Kubrick screened most of Nicholson's previous work. "In some, he played a down person, measured, slow. We decided he was more interesting up—as an active, voluble person, like the role he played in 'One Flew Over the Cuckoo's Nest,' rather than as a contemplative, brooding person. Luckily, our character was driven and energetic. […]

"We had trouble getting a voice for Jack. Jack Nicholson speaks in short blocks. It's no good having him do long speeches. […] But the character had to be a specially demanding verbal combination—intelligent, unpleasant, mordant, and sarcastic. What struck me was how well Stanley wrote Jack. Much better than I could."[80]

Johnson's phrase, "the business about the ghosts," may inadvertently reveal how little regard Kubrick had for the genre. He effectively uses a number of classic horror devices—ghosts, past lives, corpses—but their actual purpose, aside from playful experimentation, camouflages what really interested him: the conundrum of marriage, the ways in which its unique pressures bring out the worst in people. "There's something inherently wrong with the human personality," he said in a 1980 Newsweek interview. "There's an evil side to it. One of the things that horror stories can do is show us the archetypes of the unconscious: we can see the dark side without having to confront it directly."[81]

Kubrick, however, felt no compunction to provide perfect clarity. "It has always seemed to me that really artistic, truthful ambiguity—if we can use such a paradoxical phrase—is the most perfect form of expression. Nobody likes to be told anything. Take Dostoyevsky. It's awfully difficult to say what he felt about any of his characters. I would say ambiguity is the end product of avoiding superficial, pat truths."[82]

In an interview conducted by Mark Steensland for Kamera, Diane Johnson spoke of a scene from the novel that Kubrick shot but removed from the finished film. "Jack finds a scrapbook in the boiler room. […] It's like the moment in a fairy story when the hero takes the poison apple […] a mistake that brings them into the grip of evil. Before that, [the film] could have gone either way. It's [Jack's] vanity and hope to be a great writer that leads him to take this scrapbook as a gold mine of subjects."[83]

Johnson said she would have kept the scene, but Kubrick may have cut it because he wanted to de-emphasize the supernatural and put the responsibility for Jack's evildoing on the man himself. The director also chose to de-emphasize the character's artistic goals or, to put it differently, not to take them seriously.

It is impossible to believe Kubrick didn't share his thoughts with Nicholson, whose responsibility it was to locate those roiling strains within himself and bring them into the open for the world to see via a motion picture. Not many actors would willingly jump down that particular rabbit hole.

Gestation

Diane Johnson relocated to London to commence her collaboration with Kubrick, settling into a daily routine of scriptwriting—Kubrick-style. After breakfast, she was picked up by a chauffeured limousine and taken to the director's home. "We discussed family dynamics in the mornings; in the afternoon he went to the set.[84] At night we watched Jack Nicholson movies over and over again,"[85] she said.

Over and over? The director and actor were well acquainted; Kubrick was undoubtedly familiar with much of Nicholson's work. But if, at this embryonic stage of the script, he was actually researching the actor's previous films, we can be sure he used what he learned to create his version of Jack Torrance. If I were a betting soul, I'd wager he plucked ideas from Carnal Knowledge, Five Easy Pieces, and a number of Nicholson's low-budget films made prior to Easy Rider. Prominent among these are two films directed by Monte Hellman, The Shooting and Flight to Fury. Both films show how aptly Nicholson plays characters who are up to no good—who may even be sociopathic or psychotic. The character in Flight to Fury, which Nicholson also wrote, is a remorseless, smiling murderer who ultimately commits suicide.

Johnson says they divvied up the characters according to gender: she wrote Wendy, the wife, and he the husband. After she departed, however, the director made significant changes to the character she wrote, especially after Shelley Duvall was cast.

Both actors, then, were at the heart of Kubrick's creative process, though neither was present or had conscious input. Some might consider that duplicitous, but Nicholson didn't mind. In a 1985 interview, he emphasized the need for an actor to accept the primacy of the director along with conflict as inevitable parts of the creative process.

"You don't want to 'know it all' as an actor because you'll be flat. I want to give in to the collaboration with the director because I don't want my work to be all the same. I know that sameness, repetition, and conceptualizing are the acting craft's adversaries, and it seems more intelligent to start off within a framework where those things are, to some degree, taken out of your hands. It is a chosen theoretical point of departure.

"That doesn't mean I don't exercise my own taste, criteria, and forms of self-censorship. Once you've started a film, you don't become a wet noodle. You must have that conflictual interface because you don't know, and they don't know. It's through conflict that you come out with

Top: Ullman (Barry Nelson) interviews Jack for the job of caretaker of the Overlook Hotel.

Bottom: Jack laughs off the news that a former caretaker murdered his wife and little girls.

Following pages: Wendy, Danny (Danny Lloyd), and Jack Torrance drive up to the Overlook.

something that might be different—better than either of you thought of to begin with."[86]

In Vivian Kubrick's behind-the-scenes documentary, "Making *The Shining*,'" Nicholson adds, "When I come up against a director I don't agree with, I'd be more prone to go with them because I want them to have the control. Otherwise it's gonna be more predictably my work, and that's not fun."

Welcome to the Overlook

The Shining opens with a blast of jarring music over an aerial shot of a small yellow car chugging up a steep mountain road—"like a caterpillar being observed by God"[87] in the memorable words of the late critic Pauline Kael. The shot is held just long enough for its clashing images to make us uneasy: lemon-colored car… blue skies… snow-covered mountains with peaks like jagged knives.

We do not see the car's driver until he pulls up to a hotel and gets out: Nicholson, whose character is also called "Jack." He enters the lobby hurriedly and says he has a meeting with the manager. He is polite and pleasant—too pleasant. We instantly sense something false about this guy.

Nicholson is brilliant at sending mixed signals about his character and projects bravado better than anyone. Putting on a happy face is exceptionally difficult because it involves two separate acting actions: 1) knowing what the character wants or needs and 2) showing his cover-up of that want or need. The cover-up needn't be sinister but merely a face-saving stance. But it is difficult to act well.

Once Jack is seated before the manager, Nicholson ramps it up with a dazzling dance of flashing teeth, a honeyed tone and, of course, those expressive eyebrows. He is all smiles as he spins stories we soon will learn are lies. The charm offensive is of course the actor's stock-in-trade, and he uses it effectively to get what he wants. And what Jack Torrance wants, or so he claims, is the hellish job of winter caretaker at this huge, isolated, and closed-for-the-winter hotel. He needs "peace and quiet" because he's writing a novel; he's a writer, you see, teaching has merely been a stopgap measure. Nicholson plays the character as both vain and insecure—but lightly. It's too soon to get Wagnerian.

His façade slips only once, but tellingly. The manager warns that winter isolation can be daunting: a caretaker once went berserk and murdered his wife and daughters. The camera rests on Jack's blank and silent face for an extra-long moment; he looks as if his mind had suddenly been snatched. When he regains equilibrium, he smiles weakly and murmurs, "Well, that is, uh… quite a story." Momentarily, we relax. His reaction to this grisly tableau is the same as ours. We know this guy… or think we do.

But our comfort zone is soon shattered by intercut sequences with his wife and son in their Denver apartment. Danny, a disturbed child who "shines"—i.e., has psychic powers—intuits the exact moment his father is hired by the hotel. He is upset; he "doesn't want to live there" and goes into the bathroom to talk with "Tony," an imaginary friend who "lives in my mouth." He has a strange vision and faints.

A doctor arrives. While answering her questions, a trembling, chain-smoking Wendy reveals that Jack was actually fired from his teaching post and desperately needs a job. He only recently gave up drinking, after having dislocated his son's shoulder in a fit of alcoholic rage. She's clearly terrified, yet halfheartedly defends him. The juxtaposition of these two scenes alerts us to the film's true subject: marriage. It might also be regarded as advice: don't believe everything you see or hear. Funnily, most US critics didn't get that when the film first opened. It was "the business about the ghosts" that enthralled them and kept them from seeing the forest for the trees.

After the deeply unsettling opening scenes, the movie begins anew—with equally dramatic music and another aerial shot of sharp peaks and the yellow car. A quick cut to the interior shows a very different Jack at the wheel. Instead of the showy smile he flashed to hotel personnel, his lips are pinched, his face grim. Even his voice sounds different when he admonishes his hungry child: "You should've eaten your breakfast." This is the first sign of the character's oncoming schizoid split—subtle but discernible in the actor's face.

Jack Nicholson has one of the most expressive faces in modern cinema—perhaps *the* most expressive if one excludes comics such as Jerry Lewis, Jim Carrey, and Eddie Murphy. He's a *physical* actor who communicates with his face and body, as opposed to the late John Gielgud, for example, who communicated primarily via his remarkable voice.

Nicholson's particular gift for facial and body language is useful as a kind of road map or alternate narrative to the main storyline—if one pays close attention. Moviegoers typically hang on to the plot as a guide wire, but *The Shining*'s plot is sparse, just a few lines, really. Nicholson's metamorphosis is the path by which we see into the tortured soul of Jack Torrance. It's all there, for those who aren't enthralled by "the business of the ghosts."

Domesticity as Crucible

One could characterize *The Shining* as beginning yet a third time after the hotel staff has departed and the family of three is alone in the huge hotel. Jack's anger at his wife and resentment toward his son—for reasons never provided, if indeed there are actual reasons—begin as a slow boil and escalate with anxiety-provoking inevitability.

At a certain point, he devolves into what would clinically be called "psychosis"—a total split with reality. Nicholson calibrates these scenes quite subtly until the very last part of the film, when his performance goes over the top and becomes almost a burlesque. This section of the film received the most trenchant criticism when it was first released.

The Shining is structured in blocks, or movements, separated by intertitles. The first that appears after the hotel staff has left says "A Month Later." It's midday, but Jack is just waking up. He has shockingly deteriorated and looks quite strange, as if he has been drugged. "I suppose I ought to try to do some writing first," he groans when his wife asks him to take her on a walk after breakfast. Right then we know this man is not a writer. Maybe he is "blocked" or tangled in a romantic fantasy about being an author. Either way, he has set for himself an unattainable goal, a notion reinforced a scene or two later when we enter the enormous lobby where he has set up his "office." He's tossing a tennis ball against the wall—ferociously—again and again. The typewriter sits unused.

Some days later, he blows up at Wendy when she enters to inform him of an impending storm. "Get the fuck out of here!" A series of scenes that follow depict what would today be characterized as "domestic abuse" and are hard to watch, especially for women. Neither Jack holds back—

character nor actor. The husband's behavior toward his wife is hostile and threatening, not to mention unwarranted, and his language coarse. Since Kubrick didn't place much importance on dialogue, he allowed the actors to improvise. Nicholson said he unearthed some of the lines from memories of an earlier time in his life, when he was married and writing screenplays in his home and would blow up if his wife interrupted him. It isn't surprising they subsequently divorced.

One of the film's most chilling scenes takes place after Wendy and Danny are displaced to the lobby "office" so Jack can sleep undisturbed. Danny returns to the bedroom to retrieve a toy and discovers his father awake, slumped on the side of the bed. His appearance is scary but his voice gentle as he invites the child to sit on his knee. But Jack's gentle demeanor is misleading. Even though he knows the child is miserable, he asks if he's "having a good time?" Frightened, the child says "yes"—then asks if his father likes the hotel. "I love it. […] I want you to like it here. I wish we could stay here forever and ever and ever," he says, cruelly. The child then articulates the fear at the forefront of his mind: "You would never hurt Mommy and me, would you?" This precipitates a total meltdown on Jack's part, in which he blames Wendy for instigating the question.

The bedroom scene is a superb example of Nicholson's ability to effect split-second changes in feeling and intent—"beats," in acting lingo.

What makes the shifts so difficult is achieving
them while maintaining an overall sense of
bewilderment and despair. Nicholson's face asks
"What's happening to me?" as he struggles to
connect with Danny and, indeed, with himself. It
is one of Nicholson's most completely achieved
scenes—and possibly the quietest.

There is really only one tender moment
between husband and wife in the entire film—
and it is short-lived. Wendy is in the basement
taking care of chores when she hears strange
sounds coming from the lobby. She runs upstairs
to discover Jack emerging from a nightmare. He
says he dreamed that he killed her and Danny. "I
didn't just kill you. I cut you up into little pieces."
He cries out as if to the heavens, "Oh my God, I
must be losing my mind!" Nicholson plays the
moment straight and true; he communicates
real pain. Wendy is sympathetic, until Danny
enters with visible bruises—her moment of truth.
Accusing Jack of causing the bruises, she picks up
the child and leaves.

This is the only time Wendy unambiguously
challenges Jack, and it catapults Jack into a frenzy,
revealing the depths of his dependence on her.
Shaking with rage, he leaves his "office" and walks
quickly toward the bar in the darkened ballroom.
Suddenly it is filled with light, and partygoers.
A bartender magically materializes. This is the
first appearance of Jack's "collaborators"—
apparitions who incite him to murder his family.

Nicholson makes an "adjustment"—an acting
term—to the character's new reality by altering
his body language—making him stiff and jerky,
puppetlike, as if he were being controlled by
invisible strings. His facial expressions, likewise,
become less those of an ordinary human being and
more masklike. Nicholson attacks these scenes
with all the tools of his craft, aided immeasurably
by the lighting, which is often placed below his
face. We get the malicious grin, skeptical eyebrows
and, above all, demonic energy. He's funny,
sometimes, but mostly terrifying—so forcefully
does he live in the moment.

By contrast, Wendy comes across as utterly
inept, scattered and cartoonlike—unable to cope
with what's going on. All the more surprising,
then, when she shows up on a staircase with a
baseball bat, swinging it wildly to prevent Jack
from coming any closer. The film turns at that
moment. The bat provides us with a modicum
of hope, though her haplessness keeps us on the
edge of our seats.

Despite her feeble swings, after Jack threatens
her—"I'm not gonna hurt ya… I'm just gonna
bash your brains in!"—the meek wife lands
a couple of hits, one on his hand and another
on his head. Jack tumbles down the stairs, the
fall immobilizing him. Wendy drags him to the
kitchen and locks him in a walk-in refrigerator.

Soon we hear the echoing voice of Grady, the
murderous former caretaker and another of Jack's

Opposite: The ghostly Delbert
Grady (Philip Stone) tells Jack,
"You've always been the
caretaker."

Jack begins his rampage.

"collaborators," making Jack pledge to "take care of the business" of killing his wife and son. Grady: "Your wife appears to be stronger than we imagined, Mr. Torrance… somewhat more resourceful. She seems to have got the better of you." Jack: "For the moment, Mr. Grady. Only for the moment." Grady: "I fear you will have to deal with this matter in the harshest possible way, Mr. Torrance… I fear that is the only thing to do." Jack: "There's nothing I look forward to with greater pleasure, Mr. Grady." Grady: "You give your word on that, do you, Mr. Torrance?" Jack: "I give you my word." At that, Jack hears the lock click open.

Path to the Maze

The second half of *The Shining* is far less nuanced than the first and more obviously dependent on genre conventions—blood gushing from an elevator, a rotting corpse, apparitions. Duvall resembles—perhaps deliberately—the figure in Munch's famous painting *The Scream*. Nicholson's performance becomes lurid, blatantly misogynistic, and campy. We the audience start to lose the ability to differentiate between actor and character, unconsciously blaming the performer for the character's heinous acts—for making us so uncomfortable.

What caused this drastic escalation? Much has been written about the sheer number of takes Kubrick did. Shelley Duvall as Wendy had to move up and down the staircase swinging a bat over thirty times. An early scene with the cook, Hallorann (Scatman Crothers), was shot a world record 148 times. The scene toward the end, when Jack murders Hallorann, was redone forty times before Nicholson reportedly asked Kubrick to quit for the day. He and Crothers were friends, and Crothers—almost seventy years old at the time—was near exhaustion. There can be no doubt that repetition of takes to this degree depletes actors of their creative juices; it is debilitating. While the film was still being shot, the press in both England and the US ran stories about the actors' morale and mental health. Duvall suffered something close to a breakdown and had to withdraw for several weeks to recover.

Some have attributed Kubrick's actions to malice or megalomania, but it's just as possible he pushed his actors for artistic reasons of his own. *The Shining* was shot chronologically, but the script was ever-changing—a sure sign of struggle within the filmmaker. Kubrick was seeing dailies and probably an assemblage; he knew what he had. It is possible he experienced a crisis of confidence in his original concept. Perhaps Jack's abuse of Wendy was so disturbing he feared the film would devolve into a kitchen-sink depiction of domestic abuse, instead of a Grimm's fairy tale

If Jack Nicholson had lived in Paris circa 1920, he might have been a star of Le Théâtre du Grand-Guignol, a 293-seat performance space in the Pigalle district that specialized in horror fare. Its patrons would've thrilled to the sight of a father chasing his young son with an ax, like Jack Torrance in *The Shining*. Everyday realism was boring. Life was hard, and a dose of terror made it bearable. Stranglings, decapitations, and eye-gougings were regularly depicted, and success on any given night was determined by how many people fainted or threw up. Today, "Grand Guignol" is a generic term for macabre subject matter and exaggerated performances. But "Guignol" without the qualifier originated innocently as a puppet character in Lyon in 1808 (*guignol* also means "clown" in English). The puppet became "grand" as he evolved into a trenchant sociopolitical commentator harassed by the police. Le Théâtre du Grand-Guignol (1897–1962) also had run-ins with authorities. Founded by playwright Oscar Méténier, its emphasis changed under succeeding directors, but it remained a place where real issues were played out in unreal settings. Similarly, *The Shining* is a near-clinical study of a "dysfunctional" family wrapped in horror clothing.

The Grand Guignol style flourished in 1920s London. A few short films at the British Film Institute might have been screened by Stanley Kubrick, who employs many Grand Guignol stratagems in *The Shining*, imbuing it with a sense of dread and abject horror. His star was not afraid to move from naturalism to the terrifyingly absurd. "I wouldn't like to be an actor if I could only be real," said Nicholson. "I like to get wild, behaviorally wild..."[i] *The Witches of Eastwick*, *Batman*, *Wolf*, and his cameo as a masochistic dental patient in *The Little Shop of Horrors* are examples of his relish for transcending reality.

THÉÂTRE DU

GRAND GUIGNOL
20ᴮᴵˢ RUE CHAPTAL

LES PANTINS DU VICE
DRAME EN 2 ACTES DE M. CHARLES MÉRÉ
MISE EN SCÈNE DE M. JACK JOUVIN

on archetypal issues. Perhaps Kubrick's idea of a "correction" was to push it ever closer to Grand Guignol—because that is exactly what he did.

These notions are sheer speculation because Kubrick never explained himself. "I hope the audience has had a good fright, has believed the film while they were watching it, and retains some sense of it."[88] But in an appreciation following his death, Diane Johnson wrote that "Kubrick had a strong, offended sense of the ridiculousness of the human being, and the futility of human endeavor. He returned to these points again and again—with the recruit in *Full Metal Jacket* [1987], everyone in *Dr. Strangelove* [1964] [...], the victims in *A Clockwork Orange* [1971]. He assailed married life and artistic pretension in *The Shining* [...]."[89]

Repeated viewings of *The Shining* make it crystal clear that Kubrick wanted to dramatize the explosive final stage of a marriage that had become hell on earth to those involved. Although it is the husband who surrenders to the "evil" within himself, Kubrick's depiction of the wife is harsh as well. She is a role-player, calling her husband's maltreatment mere "grouchiness" until his madness imperils their son, Danny. In O'Neill's *The Iceman Cometh* (1940), Hickey murders his wife because the guilt she engenders through forgiveness is unbearable. Wendy eludes that wife's fate because of her love for her son. She finally takes defensive action, but on his behalf, not her own.

It's one thing to make a scary movie that follows genre conventions of plot, music, or special effects. It's quite another to disembowel the human soul. The unraveling of Jack and Wendy's marriage—her terror and denial, his willfulness and derangement—is what makes *The Shining* truly terrifying. That's the real horror sought by Kubrick, not cascades of blood or imaginary figures who pop out of bathtubs.

From the first scene to the last, Jack Nicholson is clear about his through line—his character's main actions and their motivation—because every beat he plays nudges the character irrevocably toward a catastrophic act, the only way out he can imagine. And if Nicholson's performance lapses into burlesque in the film's second half, it isn't because he was confused or suddenly a bad actor. Having often proclaimed himself a willing "tool" of the director, Nicholson did what he was told by Stanley Kubrick.

Nicholson has rarely spoken about his experience with Kubrick, but what little he has shared speaks volumes. He once said that if you can't do what Kubrick wants, "he beats it out of you... with a velvet glove of course."[90] In a short behind-the-scenes documentary shot by the director's daughter Vivian, Nicholson has an exchange with the director's mother, who is visiting the set. "I quit using my script; I just use the ones they type up each day."[91] Then he smiles the "Jack" smile at Kubrick, sitting nearby, who merely smiles back.

6

Jack Napier, a.k.a. The Joker

Batman (1989)
Tim Burton

"I am the world's first fully functioning homicidal artist."
—The Joker

He struts, strolls, swaggers, and twirls a baton! Saunters, sashays, dances—yes! He can even do a jig while shooting a man quite dead—bang bang bang! And what a fashion plate: trousers the color of raspberries, pantaloons with playing card designs, spats, an acid-squirting boutonniere. Whee!

But the heart of this clown is dark as ebony. The fixed smile on his ruby red lips spells nothing but trouble. "I'm only laughing on the outside," he murmurs, giggling like a fiend before rushing off on another destructive mission. What a guy!

Jack Nicholson's Joker is a rare instance of actor, character, and star persona merging to create a coherent piece of cinema art. It is a stunning performance—awesome, when studied—whose impact was immeasurably enhanced by the innovative makeup and prosthetics of Nick Dudman, the fantastical costumes of Bob Ringwood, and the deepest possible level of collaboration with director Tim Burton. "It's a masterpiece of sinister comic acting. But his Joker is disturbing enough to cause small kids to run up the aisles screaming,"[92] advised *Variety*.

Nicholson's performance—ferocious, often terrifying—is so effective that many think it imbalances a film that rightfully belongs to Bruce Wayne—a.k.a. Batman. The actor was accused of usurpation—of leaching attention away from Michael Keaton as the Caped Crusader. That Nicholson and his Joker dominate the film is undeniable, but that is largely because of Tim Burton's particular vision.

Burton wished to make a dark, gothic carnivalesque[93] movie in which anarchic forces create social mayhem via satire, humor, and mockery. Instead of a having a traditional hero at the center of the action, Burton's scenario requires the protagonist and antagonist to compete for dominance: Batman versus the Joker. Such a concept requires a villain as complex and powerful as Batman. "[The Joker] is free to do whatever he wants and live[s] on the margins, like a pariah," says Burton. "His madness […] is the most extreme form

of freedom; he no longer respects any social codes."[94] In mainstream movies, the villain is foil for the hero, but Burton reversed the paradigm: the Joker would be the dynamic force for change. Batman is modest, complex, and troubled, not a roaring hunk of testosterone. The Joker would inevitably be dominant.

Masks fascinate Burton, who believes they liberate the wearer. "At Halloween, people dress up and it allows them to get a little wilder, they become something else. […] Masks are a form of camouflage but they are also a way of making emotion public. [An actor wearing a mask doesn't] have to worry about being Michael Keaton [or Jack Nicholson], [he] can be this [other] thing."[95]

Bruce Wayne understood the power of a mask; that's why he created a costumed alter ego. As Batman, he behaves very differently from the straitlaced philanthropist he presents to Gotham City. The Joker, hideously disfigured by acid, hasn't any choice but to cover or "mask" his face in order to be part of society. But there are advantages: fools and jesters have always been allowed great latitude in what they say and do; they get away with a lot, though few are as evil as the Joker.

Nicholson and Burton are natural soul mates—antiestablishmentarians whose art reflects their joys, sorrows and, above all, skepticism. The director's outside-the-box ideas suited Jack to a tee. "I believe that part of the entire theatrical enterprise is to undermine institutions,"[96] Nicholson said. Neither man is overtly political, but it doesn't take a psychic to suss out where they stand. Burton's films tend to be about outsiders and misfits, some innocent (*Edward Scissorhands*, 1990) and others less so (*Sweeney Todd*, 2007). Nicholson is identified with rebels and nonconformists (*One Flew Over the Cuckoo's Nest*, *Five Easy Pieces*) along with a generous handful of cartoony, larger-than-life figures—the Joker being the ultimate. It is obvious how much Nicholson loved playing the character. "I always try to see how far I can go, and I've never hit my head on top," he said. "Most actors are afraid to go as dark as they might, but I always say, 'Let's get really black.'"[97]

The matchup of Nicholson and the Joker was the brainchild of Bob Kane, creator of the

Batman comic strip, first published in 1939 in *Detective Comics*. The Joker came along a year later. After seeing *The Shining* in 1980, Kane became convinced that Nicholson was the only actor alive with the right juice for the role. To buttress his argument, he sent the producers an altered still photo of Jack as the ax-wielding husband, coloring his hair green and his face white. Nicholson was by then a bona fide superstar and wanted to play the part. But the studio's reservations about *Batman*'s commercial viability were so entrenched that an entire decade would elapse before the movie was green-lighted. Luckily, Nicholson still wanted to play a favorite comic strip character from his childhood.

Yin and Yang

The basic story is as classic as a fable. Bruce Wayne is an eccentric philanthropist. As a child, he witnessed the gratuitous murder of his parents and vowed to avenge their deaths. After inheriting their fortune, he established the Wayne Foundation with a mission to clean up Gotham City. In secret, he dons a cape and mask to anonymously help the helpless and hunt down the bad guys. The community calls him "Batman." His chief antagonist is a criminal named Jack Napier—called "The Joker" after he falls into a vat of acid, which twists his face into a permanent grin.

Tim Burton's concept was decidedly unconventional and became the primary reason Warner Bros. stalled in going forward with the movie. Burton was influenced in his thinking by *Batman: The Dark Knight Returns* by Frank Miller and "Behind the Painted Smile" by Alan Moore.[98] Each author was a Jungian who interpreted the Joker and Batman as reverse sides of the same coin: yin to the other's yang—dark and light.

The studio was alarmed by such esoterica. What happened to their hero? Who would the audience root for? Things hotted up further after Michael Keaton was announced as Batman. "Batfans" thought of him as Mr. Mom or Beetlejuice—an abject and lowly comedian. Warner Bros. received 50,000 letters of complaint, and the value of its stock tumbled. Burton was forced to compromise his vision or surrender the film.

Burton agreed to cooperate with a new screenwriter and a "gagman" who would work alongside him during filming, rewriting scenes and repartee—the idea being that if the Joker was funnier, he would be less scary. The studio stipulated other changes, too, which never came to pass—at least not on-screen. Many directors would have resigned or crumpled under these constraints, but Burton had made only two features at that point and had little power. He was deeply invested in a Batman movie and needed the studio's deep pockets to make it.

A Pop Art Performance

In a deck of playing cards, the Joker is the "anything goes" card, a notion Nicholson ardently embraced in bringing his character to life. "Metaphysically, the Joker was dipped in chemicals and lost his mind—not unlike the rest of society," he said. "He has had his identity melted into his brain. He flows with the corrosion, so to speak."[99]

Jack Nicholson establishes Jack Napier as a sociopathic narcissist from the first shot of his first scene. The actor's intellect and analysis invariably result in a laserlike rendering of the character's essence—in this instance a vain, dandified, and alienated crime professional, as precisely limned as a caricature by Daumier.

When we first see him, Napier is relaxing in his snazzy art deco apartment, wearing a three-piece suit and tie. Quality. His expensively shod feet rest on an ottoman, and he toys with a deck of cards as a religious man might his rosary. A press conference on the television has DA Harvey Dent (Billy Dee Williams) promising to crack down on crime and corruption so decent people can live in Gotham City. Napier sees it differently. "Decent people shouldn't live here; they'd be happier somewhere else," he idly remarks.

His glamor-puss girlfriend, Alicia (Jerry Hall), baits him about Grissom, the crime lord who is his boss. He shrugs. Grissom is "a tired old man who can't run the city without me." Before leaving, he examines himself in the mirror with tender self-regard, turning his face this way and that. The moment is completely realized. "Jack's is not a campy performance at all," says Burton. "Jack is absolutely brilliant at going as far as you can go, always pushing to the edge, but still making it seem real. He's less broad here than in *The Witches of Eastwick*. You can't play it too broad when you have white skin and green hair. He understood when it was time to bring his performance down." Burton adds that "Jack had a clear idea of the character and played around within those boundaries. [...] He's a textbook actor who's very intuitive. He gets to know the character and then has quite a lot of fun with it. He'd always question how much he should laugh as the Joker and at one point asked me if he could really go nuts in a scene."[100]

Production designer Anton Furst commented: "Kane thinks our Joker is better than the original in his strip. [...] Getting Jack was very important for the movie. [...] As soon as he said yes, there was this great motivating force behind the movie [...]. When you have an actor with that sort of charisma, it heightens everyone else's performance and sets a standard level they all had to rise to. It was mainly because of Jack that the adrenaline ran so high."[101]

Very few actors can make a comic book character feel as "realistic" as, for example,

Three Different Jokers, Three Different Eras

Cesar Romero
Batman (1966)
Leslie H. Martinson

Tall, handsome, and aristocratic, Cesar Romero was an improbable Joker, though he played the part to popular acclaim in the television series (1966–1968) as well as the 1966 feature opposite Adam West. Born into an affluent family in New York, he was the grandson of José Martí, the legendary Cuban revolutionary and poet. After the stock market crash, he supported his family as a dancer before Hollywood beckoned. He made his debut as a gigolo in *The Thin Man* (1934). Romero's Joker, an art teacher, was elegantly fey and his cackle restrained. His colorful outfits made him look like a riverboat gambler in drag and were consonant with the pop art inclinations of the 1960s.

Jack Nicholson
Batman (1989)
Tim Burton

This Joker stuck quite close to the original DC Comics character. A vain thug working for a crime lord falls into a vat of acid and is severely disfigured. Embittered, he sets out to wreak havoc on Gotham City, giggling his way through murder and mayhem. Nicholson's Joker is a malevolent clown with a weakness for style—his own as well as others'. He also likes *les femmes*, though his way of showing affection leaves them terrified. His *commedia dell'arte* style costumes and esprit sometimes make him appear like a musical comedy figure prancing across a stage.

Heath Ledger
The Dark Knight (2008)
Christopher Nolan

With the Nicholson interpretation to work against, Ledger's Joker was a much darker figure with a strange nasal voice. Without any known personal history, he dresses in black, like a goth. He is scruffy and unkempt but highly effective in his stratagems. The actor died just after completing the film and was awarded a posthumous Academy Award as best supporting actor.

Jack Napier's boss, Grissom (Jack Palance), sets him up for a fall.

Opposite: At Axis Chemicals, Napier has his first run-in with Batman (Michael Keaton). When Batman fails to save him from falling into a vat of chemicals, the Joker is born.

Following pages: "With Joker brand, I get a grin… agin and agin!"

a butcher. Nicholson does it, though his Joker is the most cartoonlike character in the entire film. "I was particularly proud of my performance as the Joker," says Nicholson. "I consider it a piece of pop art."[102]

Nicholson and Jack Palance, who plays Grissom, have only two scenes together, but they sizzle. Their characters are like distorted mirror images of each other—peacocks whose sartorial elegance signals deadly competition. As actors, they are highly complementary—Palance a tightly coiled spring, Nicholson laid-back and then explosive. Their techniques, likewise, appear quite similar, in that they are both quite specific in their action and intent. Each of them simmers with charisma and sex appeal. It's a pity they never made another film together.

Grissom tells Napier to break into Axis Chemicals to destroy evidence, but Napier resists, citing dangerous fumes. During the back-and-forth, Alicia walks in with multiple shopping bags—presumably the first time Napier realizes she has double-crossed him. Nicholson's only reaction is a crocodile-like blink of his eyes, but it may be why he capitulates to Grissom so quickly—turning on his heel and exiting to do the job.

The moment he's out of earshot, Grissom picks up the telephone to alert a cop on his payroll to the imminent break-in. Grissom wants Napier dead.

Napier walks right into the trap. A firefight ensues, and Batman floats down into the fray.

"Nice outfit," quips Napier, who soon thereafter accidentally falls into a vat of green acid. His face is dreadfully mutilated, requiring extensive plastic surgery. After a harrowing scene in which bandages are removed, Napier re-creates himself as a malignant clown with a permanent sneerlike smile—the Joker.

The scene between the Joker and plastic surgeon is staged with Napier's back to the camera, to avoid our seeing his ruined face. He tears off the bandages and requests a mirror, sobbing at his disfigurement. He doesn't blame the doctor, who is quite frightened. Rather, he pulls himself together and staggers away, laughing like a hyena. In a later scene, he asks sardonically, "Haven't you ever heard of the healing power of laughter?" Nicholson is able to convey how much of a lie this trite phrase actually is—for not even laughter can heal a broken heart. Nicholson's ability to make this monster pitiable is an astonishing achievement.

Wait'll They Get a Load of Me!

The Joker and his world represent the only splashes of brilliant, often garish, color in *Batman*, whose palette otherwise is black, gray, charcoal, and rust.

"I got into the operatic quality of the story—big, wild and strong," says Burton, who storyboarded every frame prior to the

onset of filming. "I wanted it psychological but flamboyant."[103] Since most of the film takes place at night, Burton and Furst spun their own version of German Expressionism in terms of set design, cinematography, and atmosphere, utilizing high or sharp angles, contrasting shades and colors, smoke and shadows. Gotham City became "an essay in ugliness," according to Furst, who quotes Burton as saying "'It looks like hell erupted through the pavement and kept on going.'"[104]

The Joker's amazing costumes were designed by Bob Ringwood, who may have been inspired by commedia dell'arte figures from sixteenth-century Italy. This was a type of political street theater that utilized masks representing archetypes such as the foolish old man, the devious servant, and so on. Music and dance were an integral part of the show. Who would have imagined that Nicholson could prance around so gracefully, Astaire-like, through much of a movie?

The Joker's face was created by Nick Dudman, an esteemed makeup and prosthetic artist whom Nicholson specifically requested. The process took over two hours—the goal being to allow Nicholson maximum flexibility of facial expression. The prosthetics were applied in pieces: the nose tip, two upper lips pieces, the chin, and two lower lip pieces attached to the cheeks. The pieces had specific foam densities and had to be absolutely flawless, according to Dudman.

The white face was created with PAX (*ProsAide* plus Liquite*x*) paint. The Joker's face, therefore, was part mask and part Nicholson.

The World's First Fully Functioning Homicidal Artist

The story begins anew after Jack Napier's accident. Now bitter and vengeful, the Joker is against everybody, hate being a way to assuage his sorrow. Still a man of style, the Joker conducts himself with great aplomb, as if he were wearing bespoke duds by Armani, not clown garb or a zoot suit.

Nicholson appears to be genuinely transformed by his Joker mask, lending credence to Burton's conviction that a mask liberates its wearer—even a movie star. The actor struts and strolls as if he's on a catwalk modeling the latest fashion. He is maniacally energetic, as impossible to halt as a dervish on methamphetamine.

Napier's first destination as the Joker is Grissom's office. He wears the same charcoal-colored overcoat and fedora but his trousers are the color of raspberries and his face is fully made up—like war paint. Revenge is on his mind, and he intends to carry it out creatively; he is, after all, an artist. He wears a purple overcoat and hat, his trousers are the color of raspberries, and his face is white. "You set me up over a woman—a woman!" he yells, emerging from the shadows with a pistol fully loaded. Grissom, of course, tries

to save himself, but in vain. The Joker shoots him fancifully, from different positions, cackling with pleasure. "What a day!" he says when the killing spree is over.

It is impossible to determine whether quips such as these were improvised on the spot by Nicholson or dreamed up by the resident gagman. But one thing is for certain: if the studio intended to diminish the character, to make him less scary and less funny in order to build up interest in Batman, they failed. From the scene in Grissom's office until the finale in a church bell tower, when the Joker is at one with the gargoyles at the top, Nicholson dominates the movie.

I Make Art Until Someone Dies

The second half of *Batman* becomes increasingly terrifying as Jack Napier goes haywire. A science and chemistry major, he uses his knowledge to dream up innovative ways of harming others. He electrocutes a man with a handshake; he shoots poisonous gas into a museum while his thugs ruin priceless masterpieces; he kills a mob boss with a feather pen, crowing that "The pen is truly mightier than the sword."

The horror-filled crime spree the Joker and his thugs go on puts one in mind of Alex and his "droogs" in *A Clockwork Orange*, Stanley Kubrick's 1971 dystopian saga also set in a decaying metropolis. But *Batman* may be more shocking, in part because of the imbalance between Nicholson's go-for-broke Joker and Michael Keaton's recessive Caped Crusader. Tim Burton wanted to make a carnivalesque picture, and with Jack Nicholson he got his anarchist in spades.

Nicholson clearly enjoys himself, validating Burton's belief that masks give license to be "that other thing." It's interesting to note similarities between the Joker's many disguises and the public persona Nicholson created for himself. The actor claims he always wears sunglasses because his eyes are sensitive to light, especially the flashbulbs of paparazzi. But for over four decades, Nicholson has almost always been "on" in public—his smile wide and glowing, laughter flowing, attitude sardonic, language profane and deliberately ungrammatical. Anyone who knows the man privately knows this isn't who he really is. But the persona got him through interviews and red carpet appearances he would eschew were they not contractually required. As a kid, he reportedly never let other kids see his report card lest they see his excellent grades. He has always worked hard to be a "regular guy" and without doubt brought an extra measure of awareness to Burton's concept of a divided soul.

A Box Office Record

Rereading the 1989 reviews of Batman today is mind-boggling. Many critics actually held the film's perceived shortcomings against Nicholson.

Like "Batfans," they accused him of hogging the movie. "[He] establishes an energy level that nothing else in that brooding cosmos approaches, least of all his co-star and nemesis,"[105] wrote Jim Hoberman of *The Village Voice*, and other critics echoed that view. Newspapers warned parents not to take their children to see this monster, and the film received a child-restrictive PG-13 rating.

Such reviews probably contributed to the absence of an Academy Award nomination for one of Jack Nicholson's greatest performances. Was he too scary? Too audacious and original? At that juncture of his career, he had already received nine Oscar nominations and two Academy Awards and didn't *need* another. Still, the omission is perplexing.

Fortunately, audiences made up their own minds. *Batman* opened in June of 1989 and set a box office record. Its international gross topped $300 million—more than twenty years ago. And though Warner Bros. and Burton had been at odds during shooting, the studio retained him to direct a sequel, which was even more successful. Together, Burton's two Batman films kicked off one of the most lucrative franchises in movie history. But, alas, Nicholson's Joker would never again prance across a movie screen.

A lot has been written about the amount of money Nicholson made as the Joker. He received a $6 million upfront fee, plus 15 percent of the gross up to a certain level, after which his share rose to 20 percent. He also participated in merchandising profits, said to be considerable. All told, it has been estimated that he earned over $65 million, and no one has ever suggested he didn't earn it.

7 Colonel Nathan R. Jessep

A Few Good Men (1992)
Rob Reiner

"You fuckin' people, you have no idea how to defend a nation."
—Colonel Jessep

Colonel Nathan R. Jessep is the only true Establishment figure of Jack Nicholson's career, but the actor's natural bent toward the baroque turns the character into a fire-breathing dragon from his first line: "Who the fuck is PFC William T. Santiago?"

As Marine commander of the US naval Station in Guantánamo Bay, Cuba, Jessep is highly vexed to learn that one of his an enlistees, Santiago, has unleashed a litany of complaints to the brass in Washington, DC—Jessep's superiors. Santiago wants a transfer so desperately he has threatened to report a fellow Marine for a minor infraction. Jessep, a stickler for protocol, regards Santiago's actions as unpardonable breaches—a "break in the chain of command" in military lingo. He is also concerned that this dustup may affect an upcoming promotion he badly wants.

Jessep never meets Santiago, but a perusal of his record convinces the colonel that he's a loose cannon and needs to be taught a lesson. Although his second-in-command, Lieutenant Colonel Markinson (J. T. Walsh), urges him to oblige Santiago, Jessep won't hear of it. "We're gonna train the lad […]," he intones. "We're in the business of saving lives."

With a few winks and nods, he sets in motion a "Code Red"—an unsanctioned hazing carried out by two of Santiago's dimwitted barracks mates, Downey (James Marshall) and Dawson (Wolfgang Bodison). As ordered, they roust him out of bed in the middle of a dark night, stuff a rag down his throat, and tie him up. The idea is to teach him a lesson about loyalty by scaring him, but he dies due to a medical anomaly. Downey and Dawson are flown from Gitmo to the nation's capital to stand trial. Jessep keeps his own counsel—letting the two young Marines take the rap for his egregious misjudgment.

The Navy—with legal jurisdiction over the Marine Corps—assumes the men are guilty but assigns Daniel Kaffee (Tom Cruise), a callow young lieutenant, to nominally defend them. A quick plea deal is expected, but the plan is foiled by Lieutenant Commander Galloway Demi Moore), an Internal Affairs specialist who suspects a Code Red. She insists that Kaffee conduct a full-scale investigation, which inevitably leads them to Guantánamo Bay.

The Warrior

Colonel Jessep is a decorated warrior, too confident to feel vulnerable. Guantánamo is his turf, and he is top dog, flanked by loyal underlings. Nobody doubts who's boss. Nicholson is a terrific physical actor and accomplishes the subtext via his face and body language, leaning back in his chair, gesturing with a cigar, smiling with a crocodile snap, tossing out profane pronouncements as if they had quotes around them. Nicholson is masterful at blending characterization with star charisma, when appropriate, and Jessep offered him a splendid opportunity.

When Kaffee and Galloway come down on a fact-finding trip, Jessep summons up a goodly amount of swaggering charm, hoping to shoo them off. Kaffee lets him get away with it—but not Galloway. She knows he has previously been warned about the practice of allowing enlisted men to discipline their own, and when she presses him about this latest incident, he turns vicious. Having vigorously denied knowledge of a Code Red, he needs to shut her up. The camera moves in on the actor's face, allowing us to actually observe his mind running down possible approaches. He nods slightly when he makes his choice: humiliation. Realizing that the very attractive Galloway outranks Kaffee, he turns to the young lieutenant in faux comradeship: "You're the luckiest man in the world. There is nothing on this earth sexier—believe me, gentlemen—than a woman that you have to salute in the morning. Promote 'em all, I say. 'Cause this is true. If you haven't gotten a blow job from a superior officer, well, you're just letting the best in life pass you by."

Nicholson speaks the speech trippingly, to paraphrase Shakespeare, as if recommending a fine restaurant. What gives it weight, apart from shock value, is its truth: the prevailing attitude of hostility toward women in the military by the men who work with them—including Kaffee and his cocounsel. We've already been presented ample evidence of this mind-set.

And in that awful moment, nobody sticks up for Galloway, not even Kaffee, who aligns himself

Jack Nicholson as Col. Nathan R. Jessep in Rob Reiner's *A Few Good Men* (1992).

113

with Jessep, albeit unconsciously. This further whets Jessep's appetite. Nicholson's color is high and his teeth bared slightly as he dares to reveal his contempt for Kaffee and naval officers in general, warning the young lieutenant in a "faggoty white uniform" that he had better show respect if he wants cooperation with his investigation. This will prove to be a reckless move, possibly Jessep's undoing. Kaffee is so insulted that he redoubles his efforts to get to the truth.

The Trial

The trial comprises the last quarter of the movie and is its set piece, its *raison d'être*. If Cruise is the young cub goaded into action by Galloway, Nicholson is the wily old lion ready to defend himself. He enters the courtroom with dignity, almost cooing in his initial responses to Kaffee's questions. It's a stunning turnabout from the crude, macho Marine introduced at Gitmo.

But he isn't used to being treated so disrespectfully. Kaffee's aggressive attitude rattles him almost as much as the accusatory questions. His anxiety rises when two airmen arrive in the courtroom, supposedly to testify about an airplane schedule. Actually, the men are stooges, brought in by Kaffee as part of a trick he has conjured to force Jessep to admit culpability. Goaded mercilessly, Jessep becomes so overwrought and disoriented that he finally

admits ordering the Code Red, defending himself with soaring patriotic language. "Son, we live in a world that has walls. And those walls have to be guarded by men with guns. Who's gonna do it? You? […] I have a greater responsibility than you can possibly fathom. You weep for Santiago, and you curse the Marines. You have that luxury; you have the luxury of not knowing what I know: that Santiago's death, while tragic, probably saved lives. And my existence, while grotesque and incomprehensible to you, saves lives… You don't want the truth because deep down in places you don't talk about at parties, you want me on that wall. You need me on that wall."

The trial ends with Jessep's arrest. The two Marines are dishonorably discharged for obedience in executing an illegal order—a bind that Joseph Heller would've aptly characterized as a "Catch-22."

An American Cultural Icon

A Few Good Men is courtroom drama, a type of film so popular it has become a virtual genre in its own right. *Intruder in the Dust* (1949), *Witness for the Prosecution* (1957), *To Kill a Mockingbird* (1962), and *In Cold Blood* (1967) are notable movies that center on a trial. *A Few Good Men*'s most memorable predecessor is *The Caine Mutiny*, a beloved classic from 1954 with a legendary performance by Humphrey Bogart

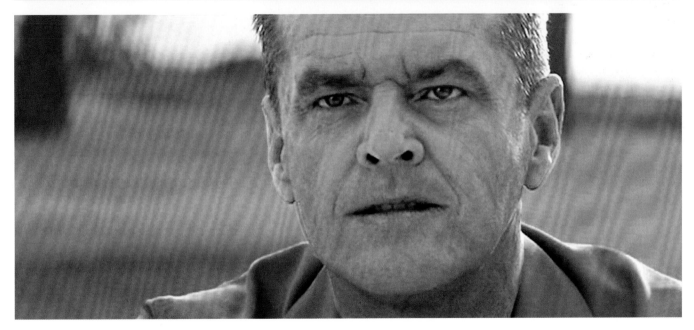

Any film about military abuse of power inevitably faces comparison to a beloved classic, *The Caine Mutiny* (1954)—usually to its detriment. That is what happened to *A Few Good Men*. "A commercially proficient movie [...] an embarrassing derivation,"[i] wrote one critic. Other pundits accused director Rob Reiner of trespassing on *The Caine Mutiny* territory, as if the older film were surrounded by a fence with "Keep Out!" signs. Certainly, there are similarities. Both films are based on real-life incidents and came to the screen via Broadway. Each is set entirely within the military, though one is by sea and the other on land. An emotional trial comprises the finale of each film.

Their most striking commonality, however, is a superb courtroom performance by the most celebrated actor of his day—Humphrey Bogart as Navy Lieutenant Commander Philip Francis Queeg and Jack Nicholson as Marine Colonel Nathan R. Jessep. Each plays a career officer entrusted with the oversight of policy and men. The men under Bogart's character's command mutinied because they believed he was mentally unstable and thereby endangering their lives. Called to the witness stand, Queeg famously toys with two tiny metal balls as a coping mechanism— unconsciously confirming their fears. Legend has it that Bogart's performance was so powerful that the crew gave him a round of thunderous applause—the rarest of honors.

Nicholson's Colonel Jessep is tricked into admitting he ordered the Code Red that resulted in the accidental death of an enlistee. Nicholson's stature among fellow thespians is formidable, but he really doesn't enjoy feeling "like the Lincoln Memorial."[k] To set a tone, he "gave a full-out performance" at the very first reading done around a table, according to Rob Reiner. The power of Bogart's performance brought the term "Queeg" into the vernacular, a "Queeg" being a delusional megalomaniac. Nicholson's taunt at Tom Cruise, "You can't handle the truth!" has likewise stood the test of time.

Despite its mixed critical reception, *A Few Good Men* was hugely successful—as was *The Caine Mutiny*. Each film received multiple Oscar nominations, including one for best picture and one for their stars. Bogie lost to Marlon Brando for *On the Waterfront* (1954) and Nicholson to Gene Hackman in *Unforgiven* (1992).

as a ship's captain removed from his command. Bogie's riveting turn on the witness stand is clearly the paradigm director Rob Reiner sought for Nicholson.

Like its predecessor, *A Few Good Men* is based on an actual incident.[106] The story was told to Aaron Sorkin by his sister, Deborah, an attorney who represented one of the Marines. Sorkin wrote a play about the case that had two successful runs on the New York stage before being optioned by Rob Reiner, a partner in Castle Rock Entertainment. Reiner envisioned a star-studded vehicle with broad appeal: Tom Cruise and Demi Moore as his stars; Jack Nicholson in an extended cameo position; a superb supporting cast headed by Kevin Bacon, J. T. Walsh, Keifer Sutherland, and Kevin Pollak.

Reiner and his partners knew the value of stars. Star power built the American film industry and is still the surest trigger to a "green light." Not every star-jammed film is a hit, but when all elements coalesce and harmonize, it's magic. Film industry folk call it "capturing lightning in a bottle." *A Few Good Men* became such a film. It grossed $264 million internationally and received four Academy Award nominations—for best picture, editing, sound, and best supporting actor for Nicholson. Cruise and Demi Moore got their share of media attention, but the spotlight shone brightest on fifty-five-year-old Jack Nicholson,

in a supporting role. He only has four scenes, one running less than a minute, but he just about steals the movie. Shades of *Easy Rider*.

David vs. Goliath

Initially, Colonel Jessep seems to be a typical "tough guy" Marine officer. But as the story unfolds, we get glimpses into the dark heart of the military crucible—a profession whose awesome responsibilities give it vast latitude to do things its own way. By the film's conclusion, when Jessep is hoisted on his own petard, shouting, "You can't handle the truth!" we wonder whether the flaw is in him or in the system.

That wasn't director-producer Rob Reiner's intent. He identified with Cruise's character, Daniel Kaffee, a recent Harvard Law School graduate living in the shadow of his illustrious father, a renowned naval attorney. Rob wanted the story to reflect his own personal challenges as the son of comedy legend Carl Reiner. He asked Aaron Sorkin to restructure his original work into a "David versus Goliath" story wherein a young man with father issues confronts and "slays" an arrogant older man whom he experiences as a surrogate parent. In this configuration, the focus of the trial shifts from the two accused Marines to a standoff between the protagonist "son" and antagonist "father": Cruise versus Nicholson. What a match!

But the David–Goliath analogy would prove to be flawed. In the Bible story, Goliath is a bully and blowhard—more than nine feet tall and protected by armor. David is slight in size; his only weapon is a slingshot and stones. Spotting an opening in Goliath's armor, near his temple, he lands a stone that knocks Goliath down, after which David seizes the giant's sword and beheads him.

Kaffee, by contrast, is a privileged young fellow with a chip on his shoulder and no real moral core. He would have blithely sent the two Marines to prison had Galloway not prevented it. And though the script tries to show him becoming a bigger, better person, we don't really believe it. David, fighting for Israel, slew Goliath because of his passion for a cause and his skill with a slingshot. Kaffee brings down Jessep because he was shamed into an investigation, and then by using legal trickery. His victory feels pyrrhic.

The Performance

American critics were generationally divided about *A Few Good Men* but not about Nicholson. "The role doesn't have to be big, but if it's good, and if the actor playing it is great, the results can be magically transforming," wrote *New York Times* critic Vincent Canby.[107] Other critics similarly praised the actor, among them Kenneth Turan of the *Los Angeles Times*. "Nicholson is capable of all manner of movie star brassiness, and his [...] Jessep is a treat, the kind of showy, self-confident acting that awards were made for [...]."[108]

A Few Good Men is hardly the first time a Nicholson portrait has been called "brassy" or "over the top." But there's more to the Nicholson effect than his ability to wow. Of course he wants to give Jessep pizzazz. He's an entertainer to the marrow of his bones, and making the character come alive is as natural as breathing. It is, however, his bold, multilayered performance that turns the colonel into a memorable, almost tragic figure, not the pizzazz.

Nicholson never pleads a character's case, but he does endeavor to show all of his sides. Jessep has been warped by years of military service, and Nicholson unsparingly reflects the good, bad, and ugly of his character—in effect "demonizing" him, to borrow a piquant expression of *Time* magazine critic Richard Schickel. It takes an incredible amount of skill—and nerve—to demonize or condemn one's own character *within* the characterization. It's akin to a moral act. Nicholson recognizes that Jessep transcends villainy. He carries within him the film's ultimate truth: that the military is a flawed but essential institution that operates by its own rules, outside mainstream society, and that it commits acts unacceptable—and illegal—to civilians. By the time of *A Few Good Men*, Nicholson was so skillful an actor that he could incorporate the

needs of the narrative, its themes and subthemes, into a complex performance that made up for insufficiencies in the screenplay. *A Few Good Men* needed him. By elevating his performance into a philosophical argument, Jessep becomes the catalyst that gives the film its heft.

Nicholson is visually isolated throughout the film, a schema that feels exactly right. Jessep is indeed a man alone. In the opening scenes at Guantánamo Bay, a combination of medium shots and strategic close-ups accentuate what the actor is delivering in performance. Jessep is always jockeying for the dominant position in a room, and Reiner shows him achieving it with the occasional master shot that incorporates other players, showing them bowing and scraping to Jessep like servants to a feudal lord. No wonder he feels unassailable.

But the style changes radically for the trial. Upon entering the courtroom, Jessep is shown full-body, wearing his dress uniform, his chest covered with medals. But after he takes the witness stand, the camera scrutinizes him like an insect under a microscope. He is stuck in a chair, so the camera moves around him, magnifying his belligerence and egoism—and revealing the exact moment he realizes he's in trouble. It moves in close... backs off... zooms to a close-up and then an extreme close-up as Jessep's face fills the screen. Cruise is treated similarly, but unlike Nicholson's, his is not a tactile presence.
We don't feel his emotion as we do Nicholson's.

When Jessep stumbles off the witness stand, bewildered, humiliated, and scared, we feel pity. The camera hovers close beside him, almost protectively. It often rests upon his face, especially his eyes, separating him from his uniform, medals, position—almost from his gender. At that moment, he is simply a wounded man. Nicholson and the filmmakers make sure we know that despite his dastardly actions, he's still a human being. It is a masterful sequence, a close collaboration of actor, director, cinematographer (Robert Richardson), and editor (Robert Leighton), all of whom were nominated for Oscars.

The nature of Nicholson's work is often underappreciated or misperceived because film culture is biased on the side of realism. Unless the character is a Muppet, puppet, or technological wonder, he or she is supposed to look like a snapshot—real life. "You can knock yourself out trying to be 'real,' but 'real' isn't always interesting," Nicholson said, paraphrasing Stanley Kubrick.[109]

Nicholson can perform realism, but it isn't his best or truest self because it doesn't allow for the play of his imagination. It is interesting to compare his work in two military pictures because they trace the arc of his artistic development. Several critics described Jessep as "the warped flip side of his Navy signalman in *The Last Detail*."[110] The film, directed by Hal Ashby from a script by

Once he takes the stand, the camera closes in on Jessep, scrutinizing him and diminishing his power.

Director Rob Reiner conceived of the Jessep/Kaffee relationship as a father/son struggle.

Following pages: Despite his arrest, Jessep remains convinced the Code Red he ordered ultimately saved lives. "I did my job," he insists, "and I'd do it again."

Robert Towne, is one of Nicholson's most popular performances, for which he won the Cannes Film Festival award for best actor. *The Last Detail* was made in 1973, at the beginning of his post–*Easy Rider* career. Its style required him to work in a realistic vein and allowed full play of his insouciant personality.

But Jessep—twenty years later—was bigger, bolder, riskier, and almost airtight in consistency. It followed a decade of baroque portraitures—*The Shining*, *Prizzi's Honor*, *The Witches of Eastwick*, *Batman*—and partakes of tendencies developed in those films that owe more to Bertolt Brecht than Stanislavski. In Brecht's work, the character exists as part of the world's machinery and is emblematic of a type rather than an individual.

Brecht vs. Stanislavski

Nicholson received his early formal training from individual teachers, the two most prominent being Jeff Corey and Martin Landau. Both were influenced by Lee Strasberg of the Actors Studio in New York. Strasberg and others such as Elia Kazan and Stella Adler famously embraced "The Method" of Constantin Stanislavski, the great Russian theoretician and stage director. The actor was encouraged to plunder his own real-life emotion for a type of transference to the character. Exercises and tricks were invented to aid the performer in making his character true to "real life."

The Bavarian Bertolt Brecht was the near antithesis of Stanislavski. A playwright, actor, and director, his theories developed side by side with his Marxist political ideology and were known as "Epic" or "Dialectical" theater. Because Brecht was an outspoken member of the Communist Party, his ideas never formally took hold in the US. He was a kind of rabblerousing "preacher" who used the stage like a pulpit and his plays to carry a moral lesson. He disdained emotional realism, preferring his actors to represent the "message" of the play so the audience would think about its content and not get sucked into shallow emotion. His plays—*Mother Courage and Her Children* (1939) and *The Caucasian Chalk Circle* (1944), among many others—can be quite difficult to perform for a dedicated Stanislavskian. To my knowledge, Jack Nicholson never had an opportunity to study the Brechtian style, but he certainly knows how to shape a character within a political, philosophical, or ideological framework. While not overtly political in his personal life, he is sometimes drawn to material that has something to say—*Hoffa*, for example, a biographical film about the controversial labor leader, whom he presented with considerable sympathy.

Rob Reiner probably didn't have Brecht in mind when he set out to make *A Few Good Men*, but he wanted to make a film about ethics and morality. "Where do you draw the line between being loyal and following orders, and acting on your own when something is immoral or illegal. It's the same moral dilemma the Nazis dealt with at Nuremberg, or Calley at My Lai. And it doesn't just apply to the military. We all live in corporate or business cultures. We're all subordinate to somebody else. We all have to make decisions about what's right and what's wrong."[111]

Lightning in a Bottle

A Few Good Men was accorded a lavish international opening just before Christmas 1992. It was a hugely successful and a media *cause célèbre* because of the marketing juggernaut built around its three stars. Premieres, parties, press junkets, and photos filled the pages of newspapers and magazines, with scant attention given to what the film was actually about.

The publicity overwhelmed *Hoffa*, released within the same time frame. Nicholson's willingness to portray the controversial labor leader, who was murdered and whose body was never found, was a quiet act of courage. He is almost unrecognizable in a minimalist realistic performance—one of his personal favorites and one of his best.

Together, *A Few Good Men* and *Hoffa* marked the end of Nicholson's youthful cockiness and the beginning of a new phase of his career as an older, more mature man, of whom something different would be expected. He rose to the challenge.

8

Melvin Udall

As Good As It Gets (1997)
James L. Brooks

"As long as you keep your work zipped up around me, I don't give a rat crap what or where you shove your show. Are we done being neighbors now?"—Melvin Udall to Simon

Jack Nicholson's delight in playing a bigoted curmudgeon is the fuel that keeps *As Good As It Gets* rolling over stones, potholes, and other ruinous road mishaps *en route* to its destination as a tract of liberal piety, Hollywood-style. Never did love between man and dog resonate so winningly—though it didn't start out that way.

The man is Melvin Udall, played by one of cinema's greatest stars; the dog is a tiny Brussels Griffon called "Verdell." Their first encounter takes place in an apartment building in which they both reside—on opposite ends of the hallway. Tricked by Melvin's offer of a biscuit, Verdell trots close enough to be nabbed and then pushed down a laundry chute. "This is New York," Melvin hisses. "If you can make it here, you'll make it anywhere!"[112] Melvin didn't imagine a soft landing atop a pile of soiled diapers for the pooch, and it is only after he is forced to take care of her that cupid's arrow strikes his dark heart.

Melvin Udall has found success as a writer of romance novels, a curious choice of profession for a man who is unmarried, unpartnered, and unfriendly. When asked by a guileless admirer how he writes women so well, he snaps, "I think of a man; then I take away reason and accountability." He refers to his gay neighbor, Simon (Greg Kinnear), as a "fudge packer" and to Simon's art dealer, Frank (Cuba Gooding Jr.), as a "colored man" with "the broad nose, perfect for smelling trouble and prison food." These imaginative slurs go on for quite a while before Melvin is brought to his senses by his love for Carol (Helen Hunt), the waitress who serves his breakfast every morning.

It boggles the mind that a character who insults blacks, Jews, and gays within a film's first five minutes won an Academy Award for the actor who played him—his third, no less. An angel surely kept watch over this entire production, not just the Brussels Griffon tumbling down the chute. The original screenplay by Mark Andrus languished in "development hell" for several years, enjoying an underground reputation as one of the best unproduced scripts around. Called *Old Friends*, it was almost made with Kevin Kline and Holly Hunter under the direction of Mike Newell, but the studio got cold feet. The language? Maybe. More time elapsed before James L. Brooks, a powerful entertainment industry figure, embraced the material and successfully brought it to fruition.

As Good As It Gets was Nicholson's most polarizing film since *The Shining*, with critics leaning toward the negative. "It is some kind of twisted tribute to Nicholson that he's able to use this dialogue in what is, after all, a comedy," wrote Roger Ebert. If these insults came from the mouth of any other actor, he continued, "they'd bring the film to an appalled halt."[113] Few other critics addressed the issue head-on, lest they be accused of censorious bias; their reservations were based, instead, on the film's sitcom plot and style.

Other commentators were less timid. "Political correctness is dead," declared journalist Dennis Lim, "and movies are only now playing catch-up" by including "all manner of rudeness, meanness, or grossness perpetrated by straight white men." *As Good As It Gets*, he argued, "is a perfect example of Hollywood wanting it both ways (how can you object to the antihero's obnoxiousness if it's all in the name of redemption?) and getting it all wrong (you can if his behavior is as pointlessly vile—and subsequent role transformation as absurdly unconvincing—as it is here)."[114] The film's original rating of R was reduced to PG-13 upon appeal—a debatable decision. If on-screen hate language were illegal, *As Good As It Gets* would be arrested. Redemption is indeed this film's Mount Everest.

Terms of Endearment

Only an actor of Nicholson's stature, with a director–producer as successful as Brooks, would be given license within the "politically correct" Hollywood community to profane homosexuals and black people as happens repetitively in the first half of *As Good As It Gets*. Even the scene with the dog is disconcerting because Nicholson plays it maliciously real, eyes gleaming and looking mad as a hatter as he dumps the wee canine down the laundry chute.

Jack Nicholson as Melvin Udall in James L. Brooks's *As Good As It Gets* (1997).

Director James L. Brooks with Nicholson on the set.

Opposite: The Anxiety Disorders Association of America lauded Nicholson for his portrayal of a man with obsessive-compulsive disorder.

Following pages: Brooks and Nicholson on set with Cuba Gooding Jr. and Greg Kinnear.

What makes the verbiage tolerable is a belief—indeed, a *conviction*—that Jack Nicholson himself doesn't believe a single word his character is spewing. Audiences relish his audacity in taking risks and letting 'er rip. The actor is so loved, so *treasured*, that moviegoers hold their breath in anticipation of what he will do next.

One can't help wondering whether Nicholson took on the role as a dare to himself. Could he pull it off after that odious first act? He has often cited "sameness, repetition, and conceptualizing"[115] as the acting craft's enemies, and Melvin Udall is different, that's for sure. But the part seems slight, especially in the second half when the film becomes unduly formulaic and sentimental.

"Jim's material is very unusual. There are things that are unwritten. I always felt that Greg had to approve my character. It's him I am sort of unneighborly with at the beginning. Working with Greg, Helen and Cuba Gooding, who are not old friends of mine—normally I like working with old friends, it is very stimulating. If you are not a specialist in any field and meet younger colleagues and it just fits, that's exciting.'"[116]

Brooks and Nicholson met on *Terms of Endearment* (1983), the director's first film. "I was completely cowed […]," says Brooks. "I tried to sound like a good actors' director and I just hated myself. He said, 'You can say anything to me; put

it any way you like.' I took him at his word and he was a man of his word. So he really helped me start directing. It was about the work. For somebody who's had a career like his, to maintain his trust, it's great to be the recipient."[117]

What Brooks enjoys most about the actor is "Jack's originality as a man, a guy who thinks about life. He is the most philosophical guy I have ever met. When you're with him you want to take notes. He gives you a slant and he's very honest."[118]

Terms of Endearment was a huge box office success and won five Academy Awards: best picture, director, original screenplay, actress (Shirley MacLaine), and supporting actor (Nicholson—his second Oscar). Nicholson's inimitable portrayal of a raffish ex-astronaut is on the short list of favorite Nicholson performances for audiences and critics alike, in part because it is quintessentially "Jack." Success at this level tends to make those who are part of it friends for life. Nicholson played supporting roles in two subsequent films directed by James Brooks, *Broadcast News* (1987) and *How Do You Know* (2010). The actor is conspicuously loyal to certain directors, and tends to work with the same ones again and again if called upon. In addition to Brooks, he has made multiple pictures with Bob Rafelson, Tim Burton, Rob Reiner, Mike Nichols, Sean Penn, and, in the pre–*Easy Rider* years, with Roger Corman and Monte Hellman.

Opposite: Despite tossing him down the garbage shoot at the start of the film, Melvin grows quite fond of little Verdell.

Carol (Helen Hunt) is tolerant of Melvin's eccentricities — until he mentions her son.

Cinematherapy

Melvin Udall has been clinically diagnosed with obsessive–compulsive disorder and is therefore a prisoner in his own life. His prejudices, phobias, and compulsions are all-encompassing. His mysophobia—a pathological fear of germs and uncleanliness—makes him fearful of touching or being touched. He washes his hands multiple times every day and uses plastic utensils when he dines out. Before leaving his apartment, he locks and unlocks doors exactly five times. Outside, he zigzags down the street in order to avoid stepping on lines or cracks in the sidewalk, saying "Don't touch!" to passerbys who otherwise wouldn't even notice him.

Nicholson takes his character very seriously and carries out all of these wacky actions as fully as a first-year acting student. The epithets become funny because there are so many of them; his bizarre behavior likewise creates humor because it provides a counterbalance—punishment—to the hurtful way he treats others. Also—and this is crucial—we laugh because this is a movie and we know something's coming soon to provide relief from Melvin's nuttiness.

Melvin's nonstop verbal insults may or may not be a separate manifestation of his illness, but they are the laugh instigators. Without his withering insults, the movie's soapiness would cause viewers to slide right out of their seats, metaphorically speaking.

The screenplay structurally uses Melvin's illness to create narrative thrust. After an unsettling confrontation with Frank, Melvin goes for breakfast at the same restaurant he always goes to, where he's always served by Carol, a stressed-out hashslinger honestly played by Helen Hunt. Carol tolerates his bizarre habits, such as the use of plastic utensils, but when he makes an insensitive remark—mild by Melvin's standards—about her little boy, she goes ballistic and threatens to have him barred from the eatery. Melvin isn't so far gone that he doesn't take seriously two threats to his well-being within an hour.

Melvin's transformation begins when the dog is placed in his care after Simon is badly beaten and taken to the hospital. Little by little, Verdell inveigles her way into Melvin's heart, eroding his crust. To encourage the dog to eat "what we eat"—steak and bacon—Melvin plays the piano and sings, "Always look at the bright side of your life." It isn't long before he and Verdell are inseparable, the dog imitating Melvin's zigzag pattern of avoiding cracks when taken for a walk.

Nicholson enacts this bizarre behavior with such fidelity, and is so believable, that he was honored by the Anxiety Disorders Association of America. "Mr. Nicholson's depiction, including the character's quest for appropriate treatment, will be helpful in demonstrating that there is hope, support and treatment for these disorders," stated Jerilyn Ross, the group's president at the time.[119]

133

Other recipients include Robert De Niro for *Analyze This* (1999) and Jim Carrey for *The Truman Show* (1998).

Crises multiply like corn in a popper in the second half of the picture. When Carol is absent at the restaurant one morning, Melvin creates such a scene that he's kicked out—to the other patrons' applause. He bribes a busboy to get Carol's last name, and takes a cab to Brooklyn to find her. Money being no object, Melvin hires a good Jewish doctor to examine Carol's son, whose condition turns out to be manageable; Melvin organizes a trip to Baltimore to facilitate a reconciliation between Simon and his ogre parents, persuading Carol to join them. Things don't go perfectly, but Melvin's deepening attachment to Carol causes him to start taking medicine to lighten his symptoms. When he learns that Simon will have to vacate to a less costly dwelling, he moves the formerly disdained gay painter and his dog into an empty room of his own large apartment—the loss of Verdell is unacceptable. Lastly, Melvin and Carol kiss many times, after which they take an early morning walk to a bakery down the street.

If this shameless fantasy had lost about twenty-five minutes, Nicholson's performance could have maintained its crispness. But after he croons "You make me want to be a better man" to Hunt, we wonder if our Jack's gotten stuck, like Br'er Rabbit with Tar-Baby.

A Bafflement: Making the Movie Work

"The tone for the picture was always a bafflement for me," [120] says Brooks, who took an entire year to work with Andrus on a revised screenplay. "I was confused about the tone [which] led to a kind of humbling experience for every actor and everyone coming in contact with it. I always knew it was a comedy and that I wanted laughs, but one form made it silly and disrespectful to the people. Another form made it too dramatic. Any moment of pretension would kill the whole deal. So on the set I was the naysayer […] always searching and taking things out." [121]

The difficulty of achieving the right tone with potentially combustible material extended to the editing room. "The first half-hour of the film was the toughest," said editor Richard Marks. "Perhaps the scariest thing […] was trying to understand how far we could go in making the Melvin character—Nicholson—difficult without losing the audience. If you allow the audience to get hostile to your protagonist in the first three reels, you're kind of dead from then on." [122]

According to James Sterngold of the *New York Times*, "[B]y the admission of Mr. Brooks and the people who worked with him, he was constantly experimenting, constantly reshooting, constantly re-editing (the ending changed at least five times, by the count of one studio executive)

and demonstrating a rare uncertainty about the movie's tone." [123]

"I think this is one of the toughest characters Jack has had to play," observed Brooks. "There's something wrong with Melvin and he spends his life disguising what it is. Jack brings the foolhardy to try to play this character. He and Melvin have a vulnerability in common." [124]

Local news media reported that Nicholson was so miserable, so dissatisfied by his inability to find the key to his character that he offered to resign and allow Brooks to recast the role. Ever diplomatic, Nicholson described the experience as "unusual, because you don't normally get the chance when you're shooting to explore everything like that. We just kind of probed around. Believe me, it makes the process harder. I can't remember a part that left me more mentally exhausted." [125]. "I had to find the balance and that made it a little bit dicey. But the character is obviously not written to be hateful forever. You have to understand your character. I never found him hateful." [126]

The only difficult part of the shoot for Helen Hunt was having to absent herself from the set to shoot episodes of her hit television series, *Mad About You*. Like Nicholson, she is astute about her material, and she wanted to play Carol as soon as she read the screenplay.

"I looked forward to working with Jack, who to me was this unknown movie megastar. I knew how spontaneous he *seemed* to be. But I learned he was able to be that way because he was so thoroughly prepared. It turned out we both like to work in the same linear way. We both like to get the logic of a scene down before we shot it. We would go through the script and get the timing: Is the next scene three days later or one hour later? So it ended up that I didn't find him any different than working with someone in acting class." [127]

This is not to say that she was entirely comfortable at first. "I was nervous [about] Jack because I thought he'd be this movie star all the time. He was the opposite. He was just an actor's actor every day. He went out of his way to make me feel like his equal and his leading lady. He was totally prepared but totally willing to respect Jim's vision for the movie when those two didn't line up. I just can't say enough good things." [128]

Greg Kinnear, who plays Simon, was nominated for an Oscar in the best supporting actor category. Almost all of his scenes are with Nicholson, for whom he, too, had nothing but praise. "The man simply has more charisma than most of us are blessed with. He really has this larger than life charisma that can suck energy out of a room. Yet he is such a fair and generous actor that when he is working with you—and I don't think he knows how good he is—you feel him doing everything he can to make you as good as you can be. […] But Jack is like a

Melvin, Carol, and Simon (Greg Kinnear) take a road trip to Baltimore.

Following pages: "You make me want to be a better man."

Brooks, Hunt, and Nicholson share a laugh during the shoot.

Opposite: Nicholson won his third best actor Oscar for *As Good As It Gets*.

musical instrument that has just a lot more keys on it than most. Everything is different and it always feels fresh and always feels unpredictable and new."[129]

No Rotten Tomatoes

As Good As It Gets is not yet middle-aged—it came out in 1997—but the sociopolitical/cultural codes it violated with freewheeling exuberance now feel anachronistic. For good or for ill, the political correctness of the late twentieth century has been swept out to sea like so much flotsam and jetsam. Rap culture alone has exponentially expanded the range of once-risky subject matter allowable in a public forum.

Today, Melvin Udall's rants against homosexuals, blacks, Jews, and women of every stripe tickle moviegoers' funny bone, if comments posted to the popular website Rotten Tomatoes are any indication. The site gives each movie two scores—one from critics, another from the public. The Tomatometer score for *As Good As It Gets* stands at a lofty 86%. Those seeing the film today say they are touched by its redemption theme: Melvin's metamorphosis from ogre to near-sainthood.

This suggests *As Good As It Gets* was something of a harbinger, paving the way for raucous comedies of the new century like *The 40-Year-Old Virgin* (2005), *Knocked Up* (2007), *Ted* (2012), and many other movies that push the envelope of taste and decorum. Jack Nicholson's penchant for vanguardism, for anticipating the coming zeitgeist, was once again proven.

9

Warren Schmidt

About Schmidt (2002)
Alexander Payne

"Pray, do not mock me:
I am a very foolish fond old man […]
And, to deal plainly,
I fear I am not in my perfect mind."
—King Lear

In a different time and place, someone with vision would adapt *King Lear* for Jack Nicholson, so the actor could close his illustrious career with the kind of grand role worthy of his talent. The unlikeliness of that scenario makes all the more precious his indelible portrait of Warren Schmidt, a twenty-first-century American Everyman entering life's final roundup in despair, bewilderment, and tears.

Though separated by centuries, Schmidt and Shakespeare's Lear actually have a lot in common. With their working years behind them, their wives deceased, and their child or children antagonistic, they struggle to give their lives meaning—albeit it in very different ways. The king steps off his throne and is cast into the wilderness, whereas the more prosaic Schmidt merely revs up his Winnebago for a trip across Nebraska. Lear does have one advantage: the comfort and companionship of his fool. Warren's only confidant is Ndugu, an illiterate orphan boy in Tanzania, on whose behalf he pays twenty-two dollars per month to an agency called Childreach. The letters to Ndugu, revealed by voice-over, constitute an ingenious device for seeing into the soul of Warren Schmidt.

The film was directed by Alexander Payne, who cowrote the screenplay with Jim Taylor. They drew on two existing sources, Louis Begley's 1996 novel of the same title and an unproduced script (*The Coward*) written by Payne several years earlier. Payne's script had lain fallow until producers Harry Gittes[130] and Michael Besman brought him Begley's novel, which serendipitously had the same subject: a middle-class man tremulously embarking on retirement. Jack Nicholson was already interested, having read and admired the novel some years earlier. "*About Schmidt* is all about human behavior, and human behavior is what Jack Nicholson is all about,"[131] said Gittes, one of the actor's oldest friends and collaborators.

The actor was drawn to the story's humanism. "I think that's what distinguishes Schmidt, really. […] Schmidt is simply human. There's no melodrama; there's no device. […] Alexander's approach to the movie was that he wanted to take a very average kind of guy, and through the course of the picture, strip everything away from him, one thing at a time, and see where it left him."[132] Nicholson also noted, "This is a human movie, human problems, human aspirations, human frailties. If I wasn't in it myself I would say it is quite beautiful."[133]

The story's setting was changed from New York to Nebraska—home turf to Alexander Payne.[134] All of the characters, Schmidt in particular, are rooted in the ethos of that region, well described by another Midwesterner, critic Richard Schickel. "Warren Schmidt moves ponderously. […] What slows him is the rhythms of his region and his culture; he is a Midwesterner of the Wasp persuasion, which means he is solid, stolid and silent, except when exchanging arm's-length pleasantries with his friends. Like so many men of his class and place, he has bent himself to a job (as an insurance company actuary) that is at once dull and intricate and to a city (Omaha, Neb.) where the agreed-upon illusion is stability. […] What he is not in touch with is his feelings—in particular, with his anger. He would deny its very existence or that of any other emotion that might upset the even tenor of his days."[135]

The Void

The film opens in an office as spick-and-span as an operating room. Jack Nicholson, as Warren Schmidt, sits at a desk staring at a clock on the wall. The room is barren except for a stack of boxes filled with his papers and files. This is Warren's last day on the job; he is retiring after a long, solid career as an actuary for a large insurance firm. Yet his discipline is such that he cannot bring himself to leave until the clock strikes five exactly. It's as if he were being released from jail. His stark demeanor and the shot itself give a sense of just how bleak a moment this is.

Nicholson's appearance is astonishing. He has never before portrayed a man his own age—sixty-six at the time—and he allowed himself to be heavier than usual, with steel-gray hair, waxen skin, and a face that is masklike—devoid of expression. Critic Roger Ebert wrote: "It is an act of self-effacement that Nicholson is able to

Jack Nicholson as Warren Schmidt in Alexander Payne's *About Schmidt* (2002).

inhabit Schmidt and give him life and sadness. [...] His approach is to renounce all of his mannerisms [...]. Usually we watch Nicholson because of his wicked energy and style; here we are fascinated by their absence."[136]

The actor believes it is essential he take his public image from other roles into account when creating a new character. "I've always felt [...] that almost anyone can give a good or representative performance when you're unknown. [...] The real pro game of acting is after you're known to 'Un-Jack' the character in my case and to get the audience to re-invest in a new and specific fictional person. In that sense I do take [my public image] into account. [...] It's part of the craft. You really have to, in order to keep growing as an actor, you have to learn the devices that keep you from just relying on what works for you. [...] In the job, you've got to be *that* person in *that* situation and get to the conflict."[137]

After the scene in his office, the film cuts to Warren driving through a downpour to his retirement dinner with an elderly white-haired lady in the passenger seat. Is this Jack's... er, Warren Schmidt's better half? Well, yes. This is Helen (June Squibb), with whom he has shared forty-two years of marital give-and-take. Our reaction is identical to Schmidt's, who later confesses to Ndugu: "I find myself asking the same question: 'Who is this old woman who lives in my house?'" Who, indeed!

Though the wife is destined for demise in about fifteen minutes, the few scenes she and Nicholson have together disorient and astound us. We cannot—yet—forget the Jack of yore: the unruly, macho roustabout nobody could boss around. Helen, an unprepossessing, sharp-tongued housewife who is always cleaning *something*, calls the shots in the Schmidt household, even demanding that Warren sit down to urinate!

Jack Nicholson received some of the best reviews of his career for *About Schmidt*, but critics were as unsettled by his appearance and minimalist performance style as anyone else. "Of all the dramatic transformations Jack Nicholson has undergone in his 44-year screen career, none is more astonishing,"[138] wrote Stephen Holden of the *New York Times* when the film opened the 2002 New York Film Festival.

Nicholson has had big-name female costars in only about one third of the forty-five features he made after *Easy Rider*. He usually played younger than he actually was, so the ages of actresses such as Cher, Susan Sarandon, and Michelle Pfeiffer in *The Witches of Eastwick*, Meryl Streep in *Ironweed* (1987), or Shirley MacLaine in *Terms of Endearment* weren't glaringly inappropriate, as they often are with older male stars. Until *About Schmidt*, however, he had never been placed beside a "little old lady," and it was downright unsettling.
If Jack Nicholson isn't Peter Pan, who is he?

About Schmidt puts the lie to the Peter Pan fantasy definitively, and the choice was Nicholson's—perhaps his way of saying, "This is who I am now, no longer young or able to pretend to be." He himself staged the still photograph that became the poster—a beard of white stubble, wrinkles, a sagging jawline, with just a trace of a twinkle in his eyes. "It's sort of like what I go through when I look in the mirror every morning, although I do stand kind of sideways," he said. "[…] I think it speaks for the man."[139]

There does come a point, as the film continues, where we "re-invest"—to use Nicholson's term—in the character himself: a hardworking, law-abiding man who did everything right except allow his dreams to invade his life. The movie calls itself a comedy, and it *is* funny—funny as in "I laughed until I cried." More accurately, it is a dark and bittersweet satire of "the good life," of the consequences of always "doing the right thing" by society's standards. Nicholson said the character was who he might have become had he not been "lucky enough to wind up in show business."[140]

Fathers and Daughters

While it might seem something of a stretch to analogize a contemporary satire like About Schmidt to King Lear, the comparison actually stems from Begley's novel, whose contours roughly parallel Shakespeare's greatest tragedy, and whose fablelike tale is even darker than the movie. King Lear, in a reckless moment, gives away his land to the two daughters who flatter him most cunningly, Goneril and Regan. A heartbeat later, they and their duplicitous spouses send him packing—making the old man, in effect, homeless. Begley turns the paradigm on its head by having the daughter refuse her father's wedding gift of the family estate, setting the stage for squatters in the form of a vixen and her boyfriend who take over the property.

Property doesn't figure in the film's story, but there is a daughter, Jeannie, brilliantly played by Hope Davis, who could vie with Goneril for nastiness. A variation of her mother, Jeannie doesn't mince words in condemning her old man for the cheap casket he bought for the wife who "waited on [him] hand and foot." Schmidt vehemently denies it, insisting—without a trace of irony—there was one other casket that cost less. The father–daughter conflict reveals that the mild-mannered Warren is a controlling skinflint who wouldn't pay for housekeeping help and who forced his wife to sell her stock in order to purchase the cumbersome Winnebago now parked in the driveway. "That was her decision," he states. Schmidt and Jeannie are so alienated from each other that she has little mercy for him. She is returning after her mother's funeral to Denver, Colorado, where she is soon to be married. She expects her father to show up, if for

no other reason than to walk her down the aisle. Arrivederci, au revoir, good-bye.

Nicholson depicts his character as a kind of stubborn bulldog of a man so sure of himself—or his place in life—that he rarely needs to raise his voice or show ire. He endures his daughter's dressing-down with fortitude—while complimenting her on the sandwich she's made him. This is truly a new Jack Nicholson—on screen, anyway. "What I have always done is […] become the physicality of the person. For Schmidt I thought, what would I have been like if I had lived this sedentary kind of life. And I got into it enough to where I really didn't like it. I thought, am I ever going to be able to return to my regular self?"[141]

He also queried insurance actuaries about their profession. "They told me an actuary looks down at his own feet when he's talking to you and he's embarrassed. And if you ask an actuary what time it is they tell you how to make a clock."[142]

The novelist calls Schmidt "an odd stickler for the truth,"[143] a facet of the character that delighted Nicholson. One of those truths is Warren's intense dislike for Randall, his future son-in-law, a water bed salesman always looking for a new scheme—played by Dermot Mulroney in another of the film's superb performances. What gives the bland Schmidt a bit of piquant personality is his occasional blurt-out of what he thinks, usually at the most inopportune moment. For example, after his wife's funeral, before Jeannie departs, he urges her to rethink the marriage or, if not the marriage, at the least the wedding—put it off a bit. She is outraged.

About Schmidt becomes an odyssey when Warren impetuously decides to leave early for the wedding, secretly hoping to stop it somehow. He has an impetus to get on the road: the discovery of love letters between Helen and Ray, his best friend. Shaken to the core, he throws out all of Helen's clothing and tosses the letters in Ray's face. Ray is bereft, saying it was a "big mistake […] things got out of hand." No matter to Schmidt; he is finished with Ray.

On the Road Again

Many critics and cineastes have compared this section of the film to *Easy Rider* and *Five Easy Pieces*. It's true that many of Nicholson's prior films are replete with pentimenti—traces of his performances in other movies—that's part of their pleasure. But *About Schmidt* stands alone. Nicholson completely dedicates himself to the character, handling every moment with utmost sincerity. "I had a mathematical background and he's an actuary. It's a slight stretch of the imagination but most people are alike in most ways so I've never had any trouble identifying with the character that I'm playing. The retirement issues, what happens when the normal

Reflecting upon his collaboration with Jack Nicholson a dozen years after it took place, Alexander Payne remembers their relationship as one of mutual respect. "I think he detected in me purity of purpose and that's why he trusted me. A director and his star have a mutual duty to study each other in order to discern the nature of the film they're making. And he did that." *About Schmidt* was the writer–director's first time out with a superstar, and he was gratified to see how hard Nicholson worked to defuse the crew's reverential attitude. "He knows who he is, and he does not want to be surrounded by an air of intimidation. He was lovely. He really wanted to do a good job as Schmidt, and he confessed that he always feels quite nervous the weekend before starting a film. I phoned him the day before and said I was honored to have him in my film. Any director on earth would be gratified to have Jack Nicholson in their film because he is 'the money.' A 'yes' from Jack automatically means financing, a studio, a first-class marketing campaign." Actors are of paramount importance to Payne. "The actor is the primary vehicle of tone, rhythm, and watchability in a film, and the director's safety net. Jack told me when we started that he needed to be free. During the first week of shooting, I had to preblock the scenes due to time constraints, so I was always asking, 'Is this or that okay?' On the third day, he said, 'Look, whatever you come up with, I can justify to myself, so just tell me what you need.'" Indeed, Payne was to learn that Nicholson's command of his craft is such that "when I would give him a direction, he would do exactly that. If I erred in my direction, I would see it in his performance. I'd have to own it and change the direction. He showed me what a pro a star can be." The two men had never met until Nicholson agreed to star in *About Schmidt*. "Jack received the script on a Friday, and by the following Tuesday I was sitting in his living room. We talked on wide-ranging subjects. The later rehearsal process consisted of my going to his home and chatting, mostly about the project, but getting to know each other so we'd have an easy shorthand. I took him actuarial textbooks. One day I arrived at the front door to find it open and him hollering, Alex, come on in.' I entered and saw him standing at the top of the stairs wearing a cardigan sweater and a comb-over hairstyle. I felt very relieved as I could see he was heading in the same direction as myself." "Directing Jack Nicholson was like driving a Maserati with super tight steering."[1]

activities of your job no longer drive your day, your loved ones move away from you, and your children get older. My daughter Jennifer has a clothing shop she's opening [...] so I don't get to talk to her as much as I did a year or so ago. Those kinds of things, so there's always a lot to identify with." [144]

His approach is rather the same as Schmidt's approach to life—do your homework, dot all i's and cross all t's, keep up a good front—and Nicholson is known to friends and collaborators for being exceptionally thorough and meticulous in whatever he undertakes. How he manages to suppress almost every scintilla of his usual screen personality is his secret to keep, but he does it so well that we eventually jettison all expectation of a "Jack Nicholson" performance and concentrate on the anguished hilarity of Schmidt's existential crisis.

After several hours on the road, Warren decides it would be prudent to advise Jeannie of his early arrival. Alas, she rebuffs him, forbidding him to arrive sooner than a day or two before the nuptials. Obliged to kill time, Warren tools around the area in the Winnebago, visiting the home he was born in, now an auto parts store, and stopping in at his Alma Mater, where he is bemused to find a photo of himself on the wall of the fraternity house. He visits a museum where he examines a collection of arrowheads. He isn't bored. As Nicholson plays him, he is waking up just a little after a long, long slumber.

"What interested me originally was the idea of taking all of the man's institutions away from him," says Payne. "Career. Marriage. Daughter. It's about him realizing his mistakes and not being able to do anything about them and also seeing his structures stripped away. It's about suddenly learning that everything you believe is wrong—everything. It asks, 'Who is a man? Who are we, really?'" [145]

Betwixt and Between

About Schmidt hits the jackpot of hilarity after Warren arrives in Denver, at the home of his daughter's future mother-in-law, Roberta, played by the extraordinary Kathy Bates. This down-home hedonist terrifies Schmidt with her casual chatter about being "very easily aroused… and very orgasmic." The scenes Bates and Nicholson have together constitute farce at its finest, each playing a series of preposterous moments as "real."

Bates said "the thought of working with Jack just thrilled me," but she'd expected him "to be more of a cut-up, you know? But he's very professional. He arrives focused and works hard. I always like that when I see that in people whose work I've admired." [146]

Warren's first mistake in judgment is to revisit the subject of Randall as an appropriate husband for his daughter. He recounts a recent nightmare wherein "weird creatures" from a spaceship-type contraption tried to take her away—and they all looked like Randall! Another child might laugh or at least smile at a parent's transparent attempt to take back his child. Jeannie explodes with a lifetime of disappointment in her father. "All of a sudden you're taking an interest in what I do?" she retorts stonily before issuing an edict: he will do exactly what she says—fulfill his role as father of the bride—or return to Omaha forthwith. Nicholson plays Warren as down but not yet out: the wedding still hasn't taken place!

There are a few sequences in this section of the film that remind us of the old Jack—of his impishness and talent for physical comedy. A crick in his neck from sleeping on Randall's water bed causes Roberta to prescribe Percodan, "left over from my hysterectomy." Warren likes the effect and takes more tablets than he should, causing him to trip out to we know not where. His eyes cross, his lips drool, and his body and limbs take on a life of their own at the wedding rehearsal and subsequent dinner.

Afterward, Roberta insists he get into her hot tub. The soak does indeed seem to fix his neck and bring him to his senses. It's when she joins him, stark naked, that the film dissolves into laughter worthy of the Marx Brothers. "Here we are, a divorcée and a widower. Sounds like a perfect match to me," she says, touching his knee under the water. The expression on Nicholson's face is priceless as he jumps out of the hot tub, skedaddling over the lawn and street barefoot, back to the safety of his motor home. The image of Jack Nicholson as a chest-thumping lothario will never be the same.

At the wedding, Warren performs his duties as prescribed, looking quite handsome in a proper tuxedo as he walks his daughter down the aisle. He trips out again during the lengthy ceremony, not from Percodan but from a powerful need to distance himself from what is going on. Nicholson conveys with considerable subtlety the character's pain.

At the reception, he causes some degree of concern as he launches into a eulogy to his late wife and makes a few oblique remarks about nothing anyone can figure out. If he had seriously considered using the moment to denounce Randall and his distasteful family, he changes his mind and delivers the kind of speech expected at such a moment: trite, banal, and false.

In a conversation published in *Interview* magazine, the painter/filmmaker Julian Schnabel asked the actor how he pulled off the speech, which is a kind of soliloquy, pointing out that what Schmidt says is the exact opposite of how he feels—yet the audience is cognizant of both the lie and the truth.

"It's a particular kind of acting problem," said Nicholson. "What's interesting about a scene like

that is the actor always knows he's not going to do what the character intends to do. Over the course of the speech, he fails. But he has to believe he's not going to fail when he starts. It's made possible by great, nonliteral writing. *About Schmidt* is a comedy; it has a wryly humorous approach. It's the audience who sees how mendacious he is […] his own self-deceptions, and they're able to laugh at them."[147]

Schnabel—a friend of the actor—marveled at how "The medium of film can convey a true feeling that's outside of the words that are being spoken."[148]

Back Home in Omaha

It isn't until the film's final scene that we dare have a ray of hope for Warren Schmidt. An airmail letter awaits from abroad, from Sister Nadine Gautier, Order of the Sacred Heart. She tells us in a voice-over that she looks after Ndugu Umbo, who is "a very intelligent boy and very loving […] and he wants very much your happiness." She goes on to say that since Ndugu cannot read or write, he made "a painting" for Schmidt, which is enclosed. Schmidt unfolds the paper to find a crayon drawing of two stick figures, a big one and a little one, holding hands. Tears spring to his eyes. As he continues to contemplate the drawing, something inside him breaks apart, and he weeps.

Asked whether his tears are "of relief because he realizes he's finally made a difference or feelings of grief because he realizes how alone he is," Nicholson said he was playing someone who believes he's made a real connection and a contribution. "You take it where you can get it."

By "it" the actor surely means love.[149]

10

Harry Sanborn

Something's Gotta Give (2003)
Nancy Meyers

"Why is it you broads want all or nothing?"
—Harry Sanborn

Why, oh, why did Jack Nicholson wait until he became a "senior citizen" to make a romantic comedy? Why would such a bon vivant tarry until the ravages of time were undisguisable? Did he fear losing his mojo if he appeared vulnerable, wore his heart on his sleeve, admitted that sex is sometimes more than just a roll in the hay?

He isn't vain. His most iconic photographs show him pop-eyed, his hair on end as if electrified. Maybe all he needed was a good script, a character he could have fun with, and a costar who could match him barb for barb. That he found in *Something's Gotta Give*, a modern-day comedy of manners that skewers America's moneyed class—in this instance, the dazzling world of arts and entertainment.

Nicholson's Harry Sanborn is a high-living New York playboy, seen in the best places with a string of dazzlers who are always under thirty. That's the rule Harry lives by, without shame, though he is sixty-three. His lifestyle is ripe for a change and gets a head start after he meets a spitfire named Erica Barry (Diane Keaton), the mother of his latest playmate, Marin (Amanda Peet). Harry and Marin are planning a rambunctious weekend at her mother's beach house when Erica and her sister, Zoe (Frances McDormand), arrive unexpectedly—also for the weekend. The women are quite perturbed to see Marin cavorting with a man older than themselves. Erica starts peppering him with questions such as "What do you do?" Harry explains that he co-owns a hip-hop label called Drive-By Records. "Hip-hop?" she asks. "Oh, rap." She hates rap, and when Harry notes that "some people see rap as poetry," she quips, "Yeah, but c'mon. How many words can you rhyme with 'bitch'?" Harry winces, but only slightly.

Nicholson plays the record mogul like a banker—with dignity and forbearance, and a stunning designer wardrobe closer to Armani than Sean "Diddy" Combs. His touch is light; he breezes through the movie as if to the manor born, with sufficient *savoir faire* to look like a player of vast experience in the game of screen romance, instead of the neophyte he actually is.

The movie's literary antecedents—social satires of the early seventeenth century—often featured a glamorous rake who is sexually irresistible. Is Harry Sanborn a case of art replicating life? "Mr. Nicholson may not, strictly speaking, be playing himself, but he seems to have prepared for the role by studying a few decades' worth of interviews and magazine profiles celebrating his unapologetic libertinism,"[150] wrote A. O. Scott in his *New York Times* review. It is certainly true the actor has cunningly used interviews as entertainments, to tease and tantalize the public about love, sex, fidelity, and its opposite—open relationships. It is also true his lifestyle is unorthodox. But is Nicholson really a "libertine"? He has steadily denied being a "libertine" for quite a few years. "I used to be able to do everything. I could work all the time, never stop, and have plenty of energy left over for other things. That's no longer the case. Getting older I don't go out as much as I used to. It's not that I like the music any more or any less. What got me out there ain't getting me out there now. I still like jazz but I ain't going out to listen to it now. […] Did I like being thought of as a rogue? Sometimes, but there's another answer: It was good for business."[151]

That is inarguable. Nicholson has been a peerless star for almost half a century, but his off-screen romances have never been replicated on-screen. Had he wished, his credit list could be sprinkled with titles like *The Awful Truth*, *An Affair to Remember*, or *To Catch a Thief*—more Cary Grant than, well, Jack Nicholson. Instead, we have *Five Easy Pieces*, in which he abandons the girl; *The Postman Always Rings Twice*, in which he sullies the girl; and *Prizzi's Honor*, in which he murders the girl. Along with fifty-odd movies in which *femmes* don't figure importantly at all.

But A. O. Scott put his finger on something not generally known—the biographical roots of the two main characters. According to casting director Jane Jenkins, writer–director Nancy Meyers pitched the concept to the two stars separately and wrote the screenplay only after they committed to the project. Thus did Nicholson and Keaton conspire to satirize their own personas. Nicholson didn't need to bone up on reams of publicity he himself helped create!

Diane Keaton and Meyers were well acquainted, so Erica has Keaton's real-life speech

Jack Nicholson as Harry
Sanborn in Nancy Meyers's
Something Gotta Give (2003).

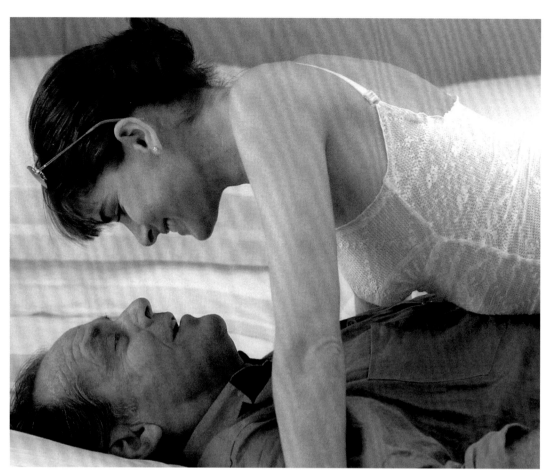

patterns and eccentricities. But Meyers did not know Nicholson and based his character largely on the public image identified by critic A. O. Scott—a womanizing, sybaritic bachelor. It isn't until the film's last third, when Harry Sanborn comes to his senses, that the Jack Nicholson of today is found: a man who reads voraciously, collects art, and dotes on his children and grandchildren.

Make 'Em Laugh

Comedy doesn't attract huzzahs as often as drama, but it's widely considered more difficult and usually practiced by specialists—performers who do comedy exclusively. Chaplin, Keaton, Laurel and Hardy, and Harold Lloyd were geniuses who rarely tried their hand at anything else. Dramatic actors such as Spencer Tracy, Laurence Olivier, and Marlon Brando occasionally worked the blithe side but didn't win awards for it. Even Tom Hanks, one of the most effective contemporary comic spirits, received his Oscars for dramas—playing an AIDS patient (*Philadelphia*, 1993) and a mentally challenged man-child (*Forrest Gump*, 1994).

While hardly a stranger to mirth, Jack Nicholson hasn't made many out-and-out comedies over the course of his career. What he has done is integrate comedic elements into dramatic material—in *Easy Rider*, for example,

The Last Detail, and *One Flew Over the Cuckoo's Nest*. He mined bizarre and often raucous humor out of horror in *The Shining*, *Batman*, and *The Witches of Eastwick*, and turned a hit man into a buffoon in *Prizzi's Honor*. His sleight of hand has been so effective that the general public thinks of him as a funny guy.

After 9/11, Nicholson made a conscious decision to look for projects that were overt comedies. *Something's Gotta Give* was the third of five comedies, including *About Schmidt*, *Anger Management* (2003), *The Bucket List* (2007), and *How Do You Know*. The streak was broken only by *The Departed* (2006), probably because he was interested in working with younger actors like Leonardo DiCaprio and Matt Damon, as well as with director Martin Scorsese.

However, *Something's Gotta Give* is the only *romantic* comedy of Nicholson's entire career. While he kisses Helen Hunt in *As Good As It Gets* for making him "want to be a better man," and he has memorable flings with Susan Anspach, Faye Dunaway, Jessica Lange, and each of the three witches of Eastwick, those encounters weren't *romantic*. A few bittersweet moments with Shirley MacLaine in *Terms of Endearment* come closest to the fairy dust he and Diane Keaton generate together.

"With Jack the script is first," said Keaton, "and when he read Nancy's script, that was the decisive moment for him. […] Jack went to where he had

The movie pokes fun at Diane Keaton's well-known conservative taste in clothing.

Opposite: Over dinner, Harry spars playfully with the two older women.

to go while filming this movie because we're telling a lovely, hopeful story for people, that there's a chance all of us can, in some way, find somebody who's our perfect sparring partner."[152]

Keaton also shared her impression of Nicholson as an actor. "As audience members, we've watched Jack do everything," notes Keaton, "and he has become a legend. I knew him many years ago when we did *Reds* together, and now having done this was a much fuller experience because I got to know him much better. And knowing Jack is like Mr. Toad's Wild Ride. You don't know what hit you half the time. What's it like to be Jack Nicholson? Who knows? 'Cause there's nobody like him, and there will never be anybody like him. Many great movie stars have incredible careers, but I don't think anyone's had as incredible a career as Jack. He's a real adventurer. I mean, he's a risk-taker as an actor, and in that way he's an artist like no one else."[153]

At its core, *Something's Gotta Give* is a mordant comedy about the vicissitudes of aging—especially for women. Keaton's comment suggests that she and Nicholson took the subject seriously. As two unattached persons "of a certain age," they each know the downside of being alone. In interviews, Nicholson has been brutally honest with media on both sides of the Atlantic, saying he sleeps alone almost every night and, worse, is beginning to prefer it. His pathos about his actual life lends itself rather

well to the theme, as if he were getting something off his chest, too. "Why is it you broads want all or nothing?," he asks plaintively, as Harry, with real bewilderment and pain.

The Noose

Nicholson plays Harry as a man whose skin is as thick as his pockets are deep. He can afford to act above it all. Watching Nicholson play dumb around these two middle-aged ladies is pure fun.

Erica: "Ever been married, Harry?"
Harry: "No, I haven't."
Erica: "Wow. Why do you think that is?"
Harry: "Well, some people just don't fit the mold. […] I guess some people find it interesting that I've escaped the noose for so long."

Ah, the noose! That jiggers Zoe's memory of an article she read about Harry: "The Escape Artist." With stiff politesse, Harry announces his intention to go home, but then allows himself to be talked out of it. He enjoys the delicious meal and is equally fulfilled by being the only male at the table.

A plain Jane who teaches Women's Studies at Columbia, Zoe goes on a protracted riff. "Never married—which, if you were a woman, would be a curse. You'd be an old maid, a spinster. Blah blah blah. But instead of pitying you, they write articles about you." She contrasts Harry's sybaritic lifestyle with Erica's loneliness: "Then there's my gorgeous sister here [… who] sits in night after night after

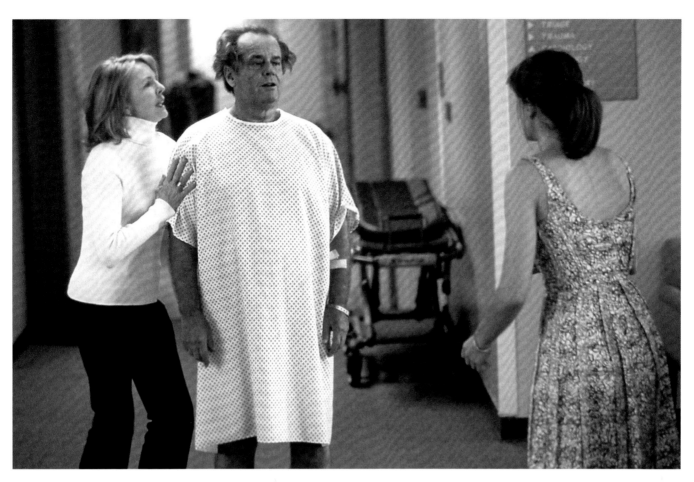

A heart attack puts Harry in the hospital, where Marin and Erica meet the attractive, young Dr. Julian Mercer (Keanu Reeves, bottom).

Following pages: Despite themselves, Harry and Erica enjoy each other's company.

night because the available guys her age want somebody—forgive me for saying this, honey, but they want somebody who looks like Marin."

Nicholson is admirably restrained throughout this sequence—as throughout the film, in fact. He plays the character mostly straight, but with tongue firmly in cheek.

After dinner, Harry and Marin speedily decamp to their room while Erica and Zoe load the dishwasher. Erica chastises Zoe for making her sound so pathetic, but Zoe stands her ground. "Thank God men die younger than us—it's the only break we get," she says. The sisters hear peals of laughter from the bedroom along with the sexually charged Marvin Gaye hit "Let's Get It On." Then, suddenly, Marin's voice: "Mom!" They rush to the bedroom, where Harry lies on the floor, gasping and purplish in color. Convinced he needs mouth-to-mouth resuscitation, Erica drops to her knees. As she gets near, Harry looks terrified—as if he'd rather expire than have her touch him. She sees his revulsion but ignores it, performing the procedure—probably saving his life. The moment is hilarious… and just a bit horrifying.

When Hearts Attack

Taken to a local hospital, Harry denies using Viagra, loudly proclaiming he doesn't "need" it when he spots Marin, Erica, and Zoe nearby listening. But Dr. Mercer (Keanu Reeves) doesn't believe him and warns that the nitroglycerine about to flow into Harry's bloodstream could kill him if the drug is in his system. Harry panics and jerks the needle out of his arm. Pride goeth only so far. Harry Sanborn wants to live!

The plot thickens when the doctor (who is "hot" for Erica and provides a romantic subplot) insists Harry remain nearby for at least a week, for observation. That, of course, means Erica's beach house. Her daughter and sister return to the city, leaving the tart-tongued playwright alone with the aging playboy. Molière kicks in during this section of the movie with classic comedy devices like coincidence, surprise, and wrongfully entered doors.

The posh beach house is large enough for Harry and Erica to mostly avoid each other. She's on one side—he on the other. She is focusing on a new play; he is lolling in the guest room, puffing on a cigar and telephoning every "doll" he knows. When she gets a whiff of cigar smoke, she barges in, barking, "I'd rather not have my freshly painted house smell like a pool hall!" Harry looks like a mildly irritated potentate in his dressing gown. "Have you always been like this, or do I bring it out in you?," he asks quite seriously. Taken aback by the question, Erica launches into an admission of chronic insomnia. Insomnia is a problem for him, too: step number one in their bonding.

Diane Keaton gets her share of ribbing in this scene. Since her halcyon days as Annie Hall, she has been gently ridiculed for prudery—for wearing gloves and imaginative outfits that cover her body up to the earlobes. Nicholson—and we do think of these characters as Nicholson and Keaton—teases her mercilessly.

Harry: "What's with the turtlenecks? It's the middle of summer." […]
Erica: "I'm just a turtleneck kind of gal."
Harry: "You never get hot?"
Erica: "No."
Harry: "Never?"
Erica: "Not lately…"

Step two happens when Nicholson inadvertently walks in on Keaton after she has disrobed. It's slapstick at its best. Harry covers his eyes with his hands and staggers backward, crashing into the wall.

Erica: "What are you doing!"
Harry: "I was just trying to find the kitchen."
Erica: "Back here?"
Harry: "I got confused… It was dark and uh… I didn't really see anything… just, uh, just your tits and a little—"

Erica screams and slams the door.

Harry later tells the doctor he has "never seen a woman that age naked before." He is peculiarly shaken by the incident, insisting it was "an accident." The skeptical doc reminds him that Freud says there are no accidents.

Later, a brisk walk on the beach produces more commonality as they agree that life passes "like the blink of an eye." Only someone who has lived long enough could make such an observation. Harry doesn't enjoy that kind of camaraderie with his "dazzlers." That's step three.

A couple of nights later, Nicholson's Harry Sandborn makes movie history by taking a pair of scissors to that turtleneck, not to do harm but because Erica is hot, hot, hot—*for him!* When he finally peels it off and looks down at her lacy bra and tightly closed eyes, he shows what a gentleman he's capable of being. "You're beautiful," he says. "Open your eyes so I know you hear me. Beautiful."

Erica didn't expect to fall in love with Harry, didn't want to, and when it happens, all hell breaks loose. A few weeks later, she goes bananas in a Manhattan restaurant when Harry strolls in with a beauty too young to vote. She runs out, pursued by a genuinely distressed Harry—the first time he's been on the defensive in thirty years. "She's just a friend," he lies. "Just a dinner." Erica declares her love and disappears in a taxi, sobbing. Harry collapses on the spot and lands back in an emergency room, where a young female doctor tells him that he was just hyperventilating. "Love hurts," she says. "Haven't you heard?" Harry tells her, "I've heard. I've just never personally experienced it." Sixty-three years of age and Harry Sanborn has

never been lovesick. Not even Jack Nicholson would make a claim like that.

Nicholson plays Harry's distress as all too real, even though it's funny. In the film's production notes, he comments: "The diminution of a man's powers is very, very humbling. You live on barbed wire and bug juice until you're twenty-eight, and there's no price to pay. After a certain point, you pay for everything."[154] No doubt about it: Nicholson feels Harry's pain.

A Man to Love

Something's Gotta Give turns to farce after Erica has a Broadway hit making fun of Harry, who is long gone from her life. Her play *A Woman to Love* is a thinly disguised account of their short romance, and features a chorus line of "Dancing Henrys" whose asses protrude from the backs of their hospital dressing gowns. Worse, the character based on Harry dies at the end of the second act!

Harry disappears. When he reemerges, it's with humility and a full beard. He has gone around the world apologizing to women he has "wronged" and now seeks out Erica to ask for forgiveness. But she's in Paris to celebrate her birthday. Ah, birthdays. Harry and Erica once made a pact to celebrate theirs together at Le Grand Colbert. What can a man of Harry's considerable means do but fly to Paris and stroll into Le Grand Colbert?

Since this is a Hollywood fairy tale, something's really gotta give. And who would have it any other way? Erica and Harry embrace as snow gently falls. And guess who croons "La Vie en Rose" over the closing titles?

Keaton received a well-deserved Oscar nomination for her portrayal of Erica Barry, but it wouldn't have been wrong to give Nicholson the Humble Pie Award for bravery in allowing himself to be as thoroughly roasted as a bird on a spit. On the flip side, the pleasure he takes in playing Harry Sanborn is evident. He lifts his famous eyebrows, makes *double entendres*, and every so often evinces flashes of the satyr we've seen in other movies. What makes Nicholson's performance so effective is that he plays the character mostly real. Many actors would mug and overstate, but Nicholson has confidence in the screenplay to properly set up the jokes, a surety born of experience. It makes the difference between a strained, self-conscious, or "hammy" performance and a truthful one that enhances the film overall. Taste also counts. His has been honed over a near lifetime of performances as well as writing, producing, and directing. Though he has one of the all-time great screen personalities and knows how to use it for a character, he doesn't fall back on it. At this point in his life and career, he is a master of screen performance and makes it look as easy as breathing.

Perhaps most delectable of this movie's many savories is watching two great stars "of a certain age" play off each other, batting the brazen, sardonic dialogue back and forth like ferocious tennis opponents determined to defeat each other. Nicholson's Harry is convincing as a doting husband, stepdad, and even grandfather. We believe it, and we are so very happy the "something" that had to give was him!

Preceding pages: Director Nancy Meyers on the set with Nicholson.

Top: Erica, Dr. Mercer and Harry at the Grand Colbert in Paris.

Bottom: A final romantic moment along the Seine.

Conclusion

It's not for nothing that Nicholson is known as just plain "Jack." The preeminent screen actor of his era—sixty-eight features, three Academy Awards, countless accolades—is so popular with audiences that his presence in a film virtually assures its financing. The broad smile and mischievous eyebrows are certainly part of his appeal. But a performer as beloved as Jack Nicholson has achieved a far deeper connection with moviegoers—something almost ineffable coming off what he calls "the Big Silver": a gutsy, hardworking and near-fearless spirit reaching out to engage, entertain, and occasionally inform them.

Voted class clown at New Jersey's Manasquan High School, Nicholson has brought that same perspective to half a century of work as an actor, writer, and director, as well as to an irreverent, sometimes outrageous public persona. A trite or untrue phrase rarely escapes his lips. He often refers to himself as "lucky," believing that his show biz success amounts to winning a "big lottery" he is happy to share with others. Only movie cognoscenti know how genuinely generous he is with friends, colleagues, and those less "lucky" than himself. Another admirable quality is his code of discretion: what happens on a film set stays there. Gossip? Only about himself.

A natural cutup, Nicholson inherited his family's creative simmerings. He could draw from an early age and performed in school, church, and community plays. After moving to Los Angeles at seventeen, he gravitated to the film world. His timing was not propitious: the studio system was crumbling and nothing had as yet replaced it. But he soon created a network of compatriots via the acting classes of Jeff Corey and Martin Landau, and theaters like the Players Ring. When *Easy Rider* gave him clout and prominence, he brought people from that time into his ever-widening circle.

The dozen years he toiled on the margins of the industry were clearly good for the artist he became, but they took their toll on a young man with a wife and child to support. He famously became a tough-minded businessman, known to strike a hard bargain in terms of remuneration, yet he lives modestly in relation to his wealth.

Overarching everything is his body of work. To study his films, to zero in on his scenes over and over again is to revere him as an actor. From the first frame to the last, he is in the moment; the most conscientious of actors; a reliable part of the narrative ensemble even as he somehow soars above it, on his own trajectory; the writer of his own cinematic history.

Following pages: Nicholson on the set of his directorial debut, *Drive, He Said* (1971).

1937
April 22: Born John Joseph Nicholson. His mother, June, allows her parents, John and Ethel May, to raise Jack as their own. He grows up in towns along the Atlantic coastline of New Jersey. Thirty-seven years will pass before he learns that John and Ethel May are actually his biological grandparents.

1954
Graduates from Manasquan High School, where he was voted class clown.
Moves to Los Angeles, where June and her children live.

1956
Makes his television debut on *Matinee Theater*.

1957
Begins taking acting lessons with Jeff Corey, through whom he meets Robert Towne, Carole Eastman, Sally Kellerman, and Roger Corman.

1958
Makes his film debut in *The Cry Baby Killer*.

1960
Memorable cameo as a masochistic dental patient in *The Little Shop of Horrors*.

1962
Marries actress Sandra Knight.

1963
Appears in Roger Corman's *The Terror* and *The Raven*. *Thunder Island*, cowritten with Don Devlin, marks his screenwriting debut.

June Nicholson dies of cancer.
Birth of Jennifer, Nicholson's daughter with Sandra Knight.

1964
Stars in *Flight to Fury*, directed by Monte Hellman, which he also wrote.

1966
Nicholson writes and stars in Hellman's *Ride in the Whirlwind*.
Stars as Billy Spear in *The Shooting*, directed by Hellman and written by Carole Eastman.

1967
The Trip, written by Nicholson and directed by Corman, connects Nicholson with Peter Fonda and Dennis Hopper and helps inspire *Easy Rider*.

1968
Cowritten by Nicholson and Bob Rafelson, *Head* brings the Monkees from TV to the "Big Silver."
Nicholson and Sandra Knight are divorced.

1969
Nicholson makes his breakthrough as Southern lawyer George Hanson in *Easy Rider*, directed by Dennis Hopper and starring Hopper and Peter Fonda. He receives his first Academy Award nomination for best supporting actor.

1970
Plays Robert Eroica Dupea in *Five Easy Pieces*

and receives an Oscar nomination for best actor.
Death of his grandmother Ethel May.

1971
Nicholson's directorial debut, *Drive, He Said*, which he cowrote with Jeremy Larner, is released.
Plays Jonathan in Mike Nichols's *Carnal Knowledge*.

1973
His role as naval petty officer "Badass" Buddusky in *The Last Detail* earns him another Academy Award nomination for best actor. He wins the award for best actor at Cannes.
Begins a sixteen-year on-again, off-again relationship with Anjelica Huston.

1974
Stars as J. J. Gittes in Roman Polanski's *Chinatown* and earns a fourth Oscar nomination.
A journalist from *Time* magazine reveals that John and Ethel May were really his grandparents and June his biological mother.

1975
Wins a best actor Oscar for his performance as R. P. McMurphy in *One Flew Over the Cuckoo's Nest*.

1976
Shares top billing with Marlon Brando in Arthur Penn's *The Missouri Breaks*.

1978
Directs and stars in *Goin' South*.

1980
Plays Jack Torrance in Stanley Kubrick's *The Shining*.

1981
Appears as Frank Chambers in a screen adaptation of *The Postman Always Rings Twice* and earns yet another Oscar nomination as Eugene O'Neill in *Reds*.
Honey Hollman, his daughter with Danish model Winnie Hollman, is born.

1983
The role of Garrett Breedlove in *Terms of Endearment* wins him his second Oscar (for best supporting actor).

1985
Plays Charley Partanna in *Prizzi's Honor*, the only film in which he shared top billing with Anjelica Huston. It was directed by her father, John Huston, and Nicholson was nominated for an Academy Award.

1987
Appears as the devilish Daryl Van Horne in *The Witches of Eastwick*, as Bill Rorish in James L. Brooks's *Broadcast News*, and earns an Oscar nomination with his performance as Francis Phelan in *Ironweed*.

1989
Rakes in more than $60 million playing Jack Napier (a.k.a. the Joker) in Tim Burton's *Batman*.
Relationship with Anjelica Huston definitively ends when she learns that actress and model Rebecca

Broussard is pregnant with Nicholson's child.

1990
Reprises his role as J. J. Gittes in *The Two Jakes*, a sequel to *Chinatown* directed by Nicholson himself. Lorraine, his daughter with Rebecca Broussard, is born.

1992
Receives his tenth Academy Award nomination for his performance as Colonel Nathan R. Jessep in Rob Reiner's *A Few Good Men*. Nominated for Razzies for his roles in *Man Trouble* and *Hoffa*, but the latter role also earns him a Golden Globe nomination.
Raymond, his son with Rebecca Broussard, is born.

1994
Receives the American Film Institute's Life Achievement Award.
Stars opposite Michelle Pfeiffer in *Wolf*.

1996
Collaborates again with Burton by making *Mars Attacks!*

1997
Wins his third Oscar for his performance as Melvin Udall in James L. Brooks's *As Good As It Gets*. Helen Hunt takes the Oscar for best actress, and the film is nominated for best original screenplay and best picture.

2001
Nicholson receives a Kennedy Center Honor for his lifetime contribution to the American performing arts.

2002
Stars in *About Schmidt*, directed by Alexander Payne. Wins the Golden Globe for best actor and is nominated for his twelfth Academy Award.

2003
Appears opposite Diane Keaton in *Something's Gotta Give* and with Adam Sandler in *Anger Management*.

2006
Plays mobster Frank Costello in Martin Scorsese's *The Departed*.

2007
Stars opposite Morgan Freeman in Rob Reiner's *The Bucket List*.

2010
Collaborates with Brooks again by taking on a supporting role in *How Do You Know*.

Page 172
Top, left: Nicholson in Richard Rush's *Psych-Out* (1968).

Top, right: As Buddusky in Arthur Penn's *The Last Detail* (1973).

Bottom, left: Nicholson and Jessica Lange in Bob Rafelson's *The Postman Always Rings Twice* (1981).

Bottom, right: As Francis Phelan in Hector Babenco's *Ironweed* (1987).

Opposite
Top, left: Nicholson as Daryl Van Horne in George Miller's *The Witches of Eastwick* (1987).

Top, right: In Danny DeVito's *Hoffa* (1992).

Bottom, left: As Frank Costello in Martin Scorsese's *The Departed* (2006).

Bottom, right: As Charles in James L. Brooks's *How Do You Know* (2010).

Page 176
Top, left: Monte Hellman's *Ride in the Whirlwind* (1966).

Top, right: Roman Polanski's *Chinatown* (1974).

Bottom, left: Miloš Forman's *One Flew Over the Cuckoo's Nest* (1975).

Bottom, right: John Huston's *Prizzi's Honor* (1985).

Page 183
Nicholson as David Staebler in *The King of Marvin Gardens* (1972).

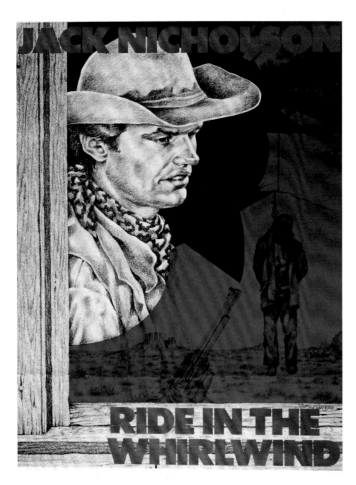

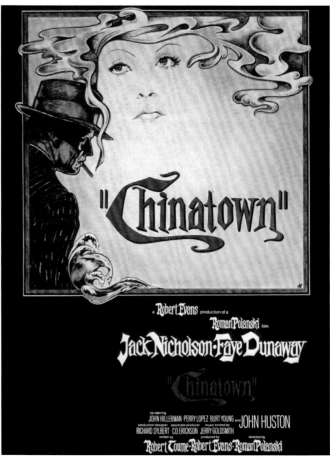

1956

Matinee Theater
(TV series)
"Are You Listening?"
(Season 2, Episode 5,
September 3, 1956)
With Jack Nicholson,
John Conte (Himself – Host),
Conrad Janis.

1958

The Cry Baby Killer
Directed by Jus Addiss
Screenplay Leo Gordon
and Melvin Levy, based
on a story by Leo Gordon
Cinematography Floyd
Crosby *Original Music*
Gerald Fried *Film Editing*
Irene Morra *Produced
by* Roger Corman, David
Kramarsky, and David March.
With Jack Nicholson
(Jimmy Wallace), Harry
Lauter (Police Lt. Porter),
Carolyn Mitchell (Carole
Fields), Brett Halsey
(Manny Cole), Lynn
Cartwright (Julie),
Ralph Reed (Joey Klamer),
John Shay (Police Officer
Gannon).

1960

Too Soon to Love
Directed by Richard Rush
Screenplay László Görög
and Richard Rush
Cinematography William C.
Thompson *Original Music*
Ronald Stein *Film Editing*
Stefan Arnsten *Produced
by* Richard Rush. With
Jack Nicholson (Buddy),
Jennifer West (Cathy Taylor),
Richard Evans (Jim Mills),
Warren Parker (Mr. Taylor),
Ralph Manza (Hughie
Wineman), Jacqueline
Schwab (Irene).

Mr. Lucky **(TV series)**
"Operation Fortuna"
(Season 1, Episode 30,
May 21, 1960)
Directed by Jack Arnold
Screenplay Blake Edwards
(creator), Paul David,
based on a story by
Milton Holmes *Produced
by* Jack Arnold. With
Jack Nicholson (Martin),
John Vivyan (Mr. Lucky),
Ross Martin (Andamo),
Buzz Martin (Bud),
Anne Helm (Edie),
Richard Chamberlain (Alec).

The Wild Ride
Directed by Harvey Berman
Screenplay Ann Porter and
Marion Rothman, based
on a story by Burt Topper
Cinematography Taylor Sloan
Film Editing Monte Hellman
and William Mayer *Produced
by* Harvey Berman. With
Jack Nicholson (Johnny
Varron), Georgianna Carter
(Nancy), Robert Bean (Dave),
Carol Bigby (Joyce),
John Bologni (Barny),
Gary Espinosa (Cliff).

***The Little Shop
of Horrors***
Directed by Roger Corman
Screenplay Charles B. Griffith
Cinematography Archie
R. Dalzell *Original Music*
Fred Katz *Film Editing*
Marshall Neilan Jr. *Produced
by* Roger Corman. With
Jack Nicholson (Wilbur
Force), Jonathan Haze
(Seymour Krelborn), Jackie
Joseph (Audrey Fulquard),
Mel Welles (Gravis Mushnik),
Dick Miller (Burson Fouch),
Myrtle Vail (Winifred
Krelborn).

***The Barbara Stanwyck
Show*** **(TV series)**
"The Mink Coat"
(Season 1, Episode 1,
September 19, 1960)
Directed by Jacques Tourneur
Screenplay Blanche Hanalis
Produced by William H.
Wright. With Jack Nicholson
(Bud), Barbara Stanwyck
(Herself – Hostess / Syd
Channing), Stephen McNally
(Bill), Tenen Holtz (Bronsky).

Studs Lonigan
Directed by Irving Lerner
Screenplay Philip Yordan,
based on a novel by James
T. Farrell *Cinematography*
Jockey Arthur Feindel
Set Decoration Edward
G. Boyle *Original Music*
Jerry Goldsmith *Film Editing*
Verna Fields *Produced
by* Philip Yordan. With Jack
Nicholson (Weary Reilly),
Christopher Knight
(Studs Lonigan), Frank
Gorshin (Kenny Killarney),
Venetia Stevenson (Lucy
Scanlon), Carolyn Craig
(Catherine Banahan),
Robert Casper (Paulie
Haggerty), Dick Foran
(Patrick Lonigan), Katherine
Squire (Mrs. Lonigan).

1961

Tales of Wells Fargo
(TV series)
"That Washburn Girl"
(Season 5, Episode 21,
February 13, 1961)
Directed by William Witney
Screenplay Charles A. Wallace
Produced by Earle Lyon.
With Jack Nicholson (Tom
Washburn), Dale Robertson
(Jim Hardie / Narrator), Mari
Aldon (Nora Washburn),

Morris Ankrum (Jonas Coe),
John Archer (Dean Chase),
Gene Roth (Sam Hargrove),
Anne Whitfield (Ruby Coe).

Sea Hunt **(TV series)**
"Round Up" (Season 4,
Episode 38, September 23,
1961)
Directed by Leon Benson
Screenplay E. M. Parsons
and Stanley H. Silverman
Produced by Leon Benson.
With Jack Nicholson
(John Stark), Lloyd Bridges
(Mike Nelson), William
Flaherty (USCG Lt. Cozart).

Bronco **(TV series)**
"The Equalizer"
(Season 4, Episode 4,
December 18, 1961)
Directed by Marc Lawrence
Screenplay Warren Douglas
Produced by William T. Orr.
With Jack Nicholson
(Bob Doolin), Ty Hardin
(Bronco Layne), Frank
Albertson (Gage), Sheldon
Allman (Billy Doolin), Steve
Brodie (Butch Cassidy), Jack
Elam (Toothy Thompson).

1962

Little Amy **(TV movie)**
Directed by Sidney Lanfield
Screenplay Norman Paul
Cinematography Dale
Deverman *Set Decoration*
Don Greenwood Jr. *Original
Music* Lyn Murray *Film
Editing* Bill Mosher
Produced by George Cahan.
With Jack Nicholson
(Jefferson City Coach),
Debbie Megowan (Amy),
William Leslie (Bill Martin),
Shary Marshall (Helen
Martin), Joy Ellison (Rosalie),
Rick Murray (Arthur).

Hawaiian Eye (TV series) "Total Eclipse" (Season 3, Episode 22, February 21, 1962)
Directed by Robert Douglas *Screenplay* Philip Saltzman *Produced by* William T. Orr. With Jack Nicholson (Tony Morgan), Anthony Eisley (Tracy Steele), Robert Conrad (Tom Lopaka), Connie Stevens (Cricket Blake), Poncie Ponce (Kazuo Kim).

The Broken Land
Directed by John A. Bushelman *Screenplay* Edward J. Lakso *Cinematography* Floyd Crosby *Original Music* Richard LaSalle *Produced by* Leonard A. Schwartz and Roger Corman (uncredited). With Jack Nicholson (Will Brocious), Kent Taylor (Marshal Jim Cogan), Diana Darrin (Mavra Aikens), Jody McCrea (Deputy Ed Flynn), Robert Sampson (Dave Dunson).

1963
The Raven
Directed by Roger Corman *Screenplay* Richard Matheson, based on a poem by Edgar Allan Poe *Cinematography* Floyd Crosby *Set Decoration* Harry Reif *Original Music* Les Baxter *Film Editing* Ronald Sinclair *Produced by* Roger Corman. With Jack Nicholson (Rexford Bedlo), Vincent Price (Dr. Erasmus Craven), Peter Lorre (Dr. Adolphus Bedlo), Boris Karloff (Dr. Scarabus), Hazel Court (Lenore Craven), Olive Sturgess (Estelle Craven).

The Terror
Directed by Roger Corman, Francis Ford Coppola (uncredited), Monte Hellman (uncredited), Jack Hill (uncredited), Jack Nicholson (uncredited) *Screenplay* Leo Gordon and Jack Hill *Cinematography* John M. Nickolaus Jr. *Set Decoration* Harry Reif *Original Music*

Ronald Stein *Film Editing* Stuart O'Brien *Produced by* Roger Corman. With Jack Nicholson (Lt. Andre Duvalier), Boris Karloff (Baron Victor Frederick von Leppe), Sandra Knight (Helene/Ghost of Ilsa, the Baroness von Leppe), Dick Miller (Stefan), Dorothy Neumann (Katrina the Witch), Jonathan Haze (Gustaf).

Thunder Island
Directed by Jack Leewood *Screenplay* Jack Nicholson and Don Devlin *Cinematography* John M. Nickolaus Jr. *Original Music* Paul Sawtell and Bert Shefter *Film Editing* Jodie Copelan *Produced by* Jack Leewood. With Gene Nelson (Billy Poole), Fay Spain (Helen Dodge), Brian Kelly (Vincent Dodge), Miriam Colon (Anita Chavez).

1964
Ensign Pulver
Directed by Joshua Logan *Screenplay* Joshua Logan and Peter S. Feibleman, based on a play by Thomas Heggen and Joshua Logan, which was itself based on a novel by Thomas Heggen *Cinematography* Charles Lawton Jr. *Set Decoration* William Kiernan *Original Music* George Duning *Film Editing* William Reynolds *Produced by* Joshua Logan. With Jack Nicholson (Dolan), Robert Walker Jr. (Ensign Pulver), Burl Ives (Captain Morton), Walter Matthau (Doc), Tommy Sands (Bruno), Millie Perkins (Scotty).

Flight to Fury
Directed by Monte Hellman *Screenplay* Jack Nicholson, based on a story by Monte Hellman and Fred Roos *Cinematography* Mike Accion *Film Editing* Monte Hellman (uncredited) *Produced by* Eddie Romero and Fred Roos. With Jack Nicholson

(Jay Wickham), Dewey Martin (Joe Gaines), Juliet Prado (Lei Ling), Fay Spain (Destiny Cooper), Jacqueline Hellman (Gloria Walsh), Vic Diaz (Lorgren).

Back Door to Hell
Directed by Monte Hellman *Screenplay* Richard A. Guttman and John Hackett, based on a story by Richard A. Guttman *Cinematography* Mars "Nonong" Rasca *Original Music* Mike Velarde *Film Editing* Fely Crisostomo and Monte Hellman (uncredited) *Produced by* Fred Roos. With Jack Nicholson (Burnett), Jimmie Rodgers (Lt. Craig), John Hackett (Jersey), Annabelle Huggins (Maria), Conrad Maga (Paco), Johnny Monteiro (Ramundo).

1966
Ride in the Whirlwind
Directed by Monte Hellman *Screenplay* Jack Nicholson *Cinematography* Gregory Sandor *Original Music* Robert Drasnin *Film Editing* Monte Hellman (uncredited) *Produced by* Monte Hellman, Jack Nicholson, and Roger Corman (uncredited). With Jack Nicholson (Wes), Cameron Mitchell (Vern), Tom Filer (Otis), Millie Perkins (Abigail), Katherine Squire (Catherine), George Mitchell (Evan), Rupert Crosse (Indian Joe).

Dr. Kildare
"A Patient Lost" (Season 5, Episode 47, February 22, 1966) "What Happened to All the Sunshine and Roses?" (Season 5, Episode 48, February 28, 1966) "The Taste of Crow" (Season 5, Episode 49, March 7, 1966) "Out of a Concrete Tower" (Season 5, Episode 50, March 8, 1966)
Directed by Alf Kjellin *Screenplay* Archie L. Tegland *Produced by* Norman Felton.

With Jack Nicholson (Jaime Angel), Richard Chamberlain (Dr. James Kildare), Raymond Massey (Dr. Leonard Gillespie), Martin Balsam (Dr. Milton Orliff), William Shatner (Dr. Carl Noyes).

The Shooting
Directed by Monte Hellman *Screenplay* Carole Eastman (as Adrien Joyce) *Cinematography* Gregory Sandor *Original Music* Richard Markowitz *Film Editing* Monte Hellman (uncredited) *Produced by* Monte Hellman and Jack Nicholson. With Jack Nicholson (Billy Spear), Will Hutchins (Coley Boyard), B. J. Merholz (Leland Drum), Millie Perkins (Woman), Warren Oates (Willett Gashade), Charles Eastman (Bearded man).

The Andy Griffith Show (TV series) "Opie Finds a Baby" (Season 7, Episode 10, November 21, 1966)
Directed by Lee Philips *Screenplay* Stan Dreben and Sidney A. Mandel *Produced by* Bob Ross. With Jack Nicholson (Mr. Garland), Andy Griffith (Sheriff Andy Taylor), Ron Howard (Opie Taylor), Frances Bavier (Aunt Bee Taylor), George Lindsey (Goober Pyle).

Voyage to the Bottom of the Sea (TV series) "The Lost Bomb" (Season 3, Episode 13, December 11, 1966)
Directed by Gerald Mayer *Screenplay* Irwin Allen and Oliver Crawford *Produced by* Irwin Allen. With Jack Nicholson (Crewman [uncredited]), Richard Basehart (Adm. Harriman Nelson), David Hedison (Capt. Lee B. Crane), John Lupton (Dr. Bradley), Gerald Mohr (Athos Vadim), Terry Becker (Chief Francis Ethelbert Sharkey).

1967

Hells Angels on Wheels

Directed by Richard Rush *Screenplay* R. Wright Campbell *Cinematography* László Kovács *Set Decoration* Wally Moon *Original Music* Stu Phillips *Film Editing* William Martin *Produced by* Joe Solomon. With Jack Nicholson (Poet), Adam Roarke (Buddy), Sabrina Scharf (Shill), Jana Taylor (Abigale), Richard Anders (Bull), John Garwood (Jocko).

The St. Valentine's Day Massacre

Directed by Roger Corman *Screenplay* Howard Browne *Cinematography* Milton R. Krasner *Set Decoration* Steven Potter and Walter M. Scott *Film Editing* William B. Murphy *Produced by* Roger Corman. With Jack Nicholson (Gino, Hit Man [uncredited]), Jason Robards (Al Capone), George Segal (Peter Gusenberg), Ralph Meeker (George Clarence "Bugs" Moran), Jean Hale (Myrtle), Clint Ritchie (Jack McGurn).

The Trip

Directed by Roger Corman *Screenplay* Jack Nicholson *Cinematography* Archie R. Dalzell *Original Music* Electric Flag *Film Editing* Ronald Sinclair *Produced by* Roger Corman. With Peter Fonda (Paul Groves), Susan Strasberg (Sally Groves), Bruce Dern (John), Dennis Hopper (Max), Salli Sachse (Glenn).

The Guns of Will Sonnett (TV series)

"A Son for a Son" (Season 1, Episode 7, October 20, 1967)

Directed by Richard C. Sarafian *Screenplay* Richard Carr and Aaron Spelling *Produced by* Aaron Spelling. With Jack Nicholson (Tom Murdock), Walter Brennan (Will Sonnett), Dack Rambo (Jeff Sonnett), Royal Dano (Vance Murdock), Jack Elam (Sam – Sheriff), Virginia Gregg (Mrs. Murdock).

The Andy Griffith Show (TV series)

"Aunt Bee, the Juror" (Season 8, Episode 7, October 23, 1967)

Directed by Lee Philips *Screenplay* Kent Wilson *Produced by* Bob Ross. With Jack Nicholson (Marvin Jenkins), Andy Griffith (Sheriff Andy Taylor), Ron Howard (Opie Taylor), Frances Bavier (Aunt Bee Taylor), George Lindsey (Goober Pyle), Henry Jaglom (Warren).

1968

Psych-Out

Directed by Richard Rush *Screenplay* E. Hunter Willett and Betty Ulius, based on a story by E. Hunter Willett *Cinematography* László Kovács *Set Decoration* James Cotton *Original Music* Ronald Stein *Film Editing* Renn Reynolds *Produced by* Dick Clark. With Jack Nicholson (Stoney), Susan Strasberg (Jenny Davis), Dean Stockwell (Dave), Bruce Dern (Steve Davis), Adam Roarke (Ben), Max Julien (Elwood).

Head

Directed by Bob Rafelson *Screenplay* Bob Rafelson and Jack Nicholson *Cinematography* Michel Hugo *Set Decoration* Ned Parsons *Film Editing* Michael Pozen and Monte Hellman (uncredited) *Produced by* Jack Nicholson and Bob Rafelson. With Peter Tork (Peter), Davy Jones (Davy), Micky Dolenz (Micky), Michael Nesmith (Mike).

1969

Easy Rider

Directed by Dennis Hopper *Screenplay* Peter Fonda, Dennis Hopper, and Terry Southern *Cinematography* László Kovács *Film Editing* Donn Cambern *Produced by* Peter Fonda and Bob Rafelson (uncredited). With Jack Nicholson (George Hanson), Peter Fonda (Wyatt), Dennis Hopper (Billy), Antonio Mendoza (Jesus), Phil Spector (Connection).

1970

Rebel Rousers

Directed by Martin B. Cohen *Screenplay* Martin B. Cohen, Michael Kars, and Abe Polsky *Cinematography* László Kovács and Glen R. Smith *Original Music* William Loose *Film Editing* George W. Brooks *Produced by* Martin B. Cohen. With Jack Nicholson (Bunny), Cameron Mitchell (Paul Collier), Bruce Dern (J. J. Weston), Diane Ladd (Karen), Harry Dean Stanton (Randolph Halverson).

On a Clear Day You Can See Forever

Directed by Vincente Minnelli *Screenplay* Alan Jay Lerner, based on a musical by Burton Lane (music) and Alan Jay Lerner (lyrics) *Cinematography* Harry Stradling Sr. *Set Decoration* Raphael Bretton and George James Hopkins *Original Music* Nelson Riddle (uncredited) *Film Editing* David Bretherton *Produced by* Howard W. Koch. With Jack Nicholson (Tad Pringle), Barbra Streisand (Daisy Gamble), Yves Montand (Dr. Marc Chabot), Bob Newhart (Dr. Mason Hume), Larry Blyden (Warren Pratt), Simon Oakland (Dr. Conrad Fuller).

Five Easy Pieces

Directed by Bob Rafelson *Screenplay* Carole Eastman (as Adrien Joyce), based on a story by Carole Eastman and Bob Rafelson *Cinematography* László Kovács *Film Editing* Christopher Holmes and Gerald Shepard *Produced by* Bob Rafelson and Richard Wechsler. With Jack Nicholson (Robert "Bobby" Eroica Dupea), Karen Black (Rayette Dipesto), Billy Green Bush (Elton), Fannie Flagg (Stoney), Sally Struthers (Betty), Lois Smith (Partita Dupea), Susan Anspach (Catherine Van Oost), Ralph Waite (Carl Fidelio Dupea), William Challee (Nicholas Dupea).

1971

Drive, He Said

Directed by Jack Nicholson *Screenplay* Jeremy Larner and Jack Nicholson, based on a novel by Jeremy Larner *Cinematography* Bill Butler *Original Music* David Shire *Film Editing* Donn Cambern, Christopher Holmes, Pat Somerset, and Robert L. Wolfe *Produced by* Steve Blauner and Jack Nicholson. With William Tepper (Hector Bloom), Karen Black (Olive Calvin), Michael Margotta (Gabriel), Bruce Dern (Coach Bullion), Robert Towne (Richard Calvin), Henry Jaglom (Conrad).

Carnal Knowledge

Directed by Mike Nichols *Screenplay* Jules Feiffer *Cinematography* Giuseppe Rotunno *Set Decoration* George R. Nelson *Film Editing* Sam O'Steen *Produced by* Mike Nichols. With Jack Nicholson (Jonathan), Ann-Margret (Bobbie), Art Garfunkel (Sandy), Candice Bergen (Susan), Rita Moreno (Louise), Cynthia O'Neal (Cindy), Carol Kane (Jennifer).

A Safe Place

Directed by Henry Jaglom *Screenplay* Henry Jaglom *Cinematography* Richard C. Kratina *Original Music* Jim Gitter *Film Editing* Pieter Bergema *Produced by* Bert Schneider. With Jack Nicholson (Mitch), Tuesday Weld (Susan/Noah), Orson Welles (The Magician), Phil Proctor (Fred), Gwen Welles (Bari), Dov Lawrence (Larry).

1972

The King of Marvin Gardens

Directed by Bob Rafelson *Screenplay* Jacob Brackman, based on a story by Bob Rafelson and Jacob Brackman *Cinematography* László Kovács *Film Editing* John F. Link *Produced by* Bob Rafelson. With Jack Nicholson (David Staebler), Bruce Dern (Jason Staebler), Ellen Burstyn (Sally), Julia Anne Robinson (Jessica), Scatman Crothers (Lewis), Charles LaVine (Grandfather).

1973

The Last Detail

Directed by Hal Ashby *Screenplay* Robert Towne, based on a novel by Darryl Ponicsan *Cinematography* Michael Chapman *Original Music* Johnny Mandel *Film Editing* Robert C. Jones *Produced by* Gerald Ayres. With Jack Nicholson (Buddusky), Otis Young (Mulhall), Randy Quaid (Meadows), Carol Kane (Young whore), Michael Moriarty (Marine O. D.).

1974

Chinatown

Directed by Roman Polanski *Screenplay* Robert Towne *Cinematography* John A. Alonzo *Set Decoration* Ruby R. Levitt *Original Music* Jerry Goldsmith *Film Editing* Sam O'Steen *Produced by* Robert Evans. With Jack Nicholson (J. J. "Jake" Gittes), Faye Dunaway (Evelyn Mulwray), John Huston (Noah Cross), Perry Lopez (Escobar), John Hillerman (Yelburton), Darrell Zwerling (Hollis Mulwray), Diane Ladd (Ida Sessions), Roman Polanski (Man with knife).

1975

Tommy

Directed by Ken Russell *Screenplay* Ken Russell, based on a record album by Pete Townshend *Cinematography* Dick Bush, Robin Lehman

(special material), and Ronnie Taylor *Original Music* Pete Townshend *Film Editing* Stuart Baird *Produced by* Ken Russell and Robert Stigwood. With Jack Nicholson (The Specialist), Oliver Reed (Frank Hobbs), Ann-Margret (Nora Walker), Roger Daltrey (Tommy Walker), Elton John (Local Lad/The Pinball Wizard), Eric Clapton (The Preacher), John Entwistle (Himself), Keith Moon (Uncle Ernie), Robert Powell (Captain Walker), Paul Nicholas (Cousin Kevin).

The Passenger
(Professione: reporter)

Directed by Michelangelo Antonioni *Screenplay* Mark Peploe, Peter Wollen, and Michelangelo Antonioni, based on a story by Mark Peploe *Cinematography* Luciano Tovoli *Set Decoration* Osvaldo Desideri *Original Music* Ivan Vandor *Film Editing* Michelangelo Antonioni and Franco Arcalli *Produced by* Carlo Ponti. With Jack Nicholson (David Locke), Maria Schneider (Girl), Jenny Runacre (Rachel Locke), Ian Hendry (Martin Knight), Charles Mulvehill (David Robertson), Steven Berkoff (Stephen).

The Fortune

Directed by Mike Nichols *Screenplay* Carole Eastman (as Adrien Joyce) *Cinematography* John A. Alonzo *Set Decoration* George Gaines *Original Music* José Padilla and David Shire *Film Editing* Stu Linder *Produced by* Don Devlin and Mike Nichols. With Jack Nicholson (Oscar), Stockard Channing (Freddie), Warren Beatty (Nicky), Florence Stanley (Mrs. Gould).

One Flew Over the Cuckoo's Net

Directed by Miloš Forman *Screenplay* Lawrence Hauben and Bo Goldman, based on a play by Dale Wasserman,

which was itself based on a novel by Ken Kesey *Cinematography* Haskell Wexler *Original Music* Jack Nitzsche *Film Editing* Sheldon Kahn and Lynzee Klingman *Produced by* Michael Douglas and Saul Zaentz. With Jack Nicholson (Randle Patrick McMurphy), Michael Berryman (Ellis), Peter Brocco (Col. Matterson), Will Sampson (Chief Bromden), Danny DeVito (Martini), Sydney Lassick (Cheswick), William Redfield (Harding), Brad Dourif (Billy Bibbit), Christopher Lloyd (Taber), Louise Fletcher (Nurse Ratched), Dr. Dean R. Brooks (Dr. Spivey).

1976

The Missouri Breaks

Directed by Arthur Penn *Screenplay* Thomas McGuane and Robert Towne (uncredited) *Cinematography* Michael C. Butler *Set Decoration* Marvin March *Original Music* John Williams *Film Editing* Gerald B. Greenberg, Stephen A. Rotter, and Dede Allen *Produced by* Elliott Kastner and Robert M. Sherman. With Jack Nicholson (Tom Logan), Marlon Brando (Robert E. Lee Clayton), Randy Quaid (Little Tod), Kathleen Lloyd (Jane Braxton), John McLiam (David Braxton), Frederic Forrest (Cary).

The Last Tycoon

Directed by Elia Kazan *Screenplay* Harold Pinter, based on a novel by Francis Scott Fitzgerald *Cinematography* Victor J. Kemper *Set Decoration* Jerry Wunderlich *Original Music* Maurice Jarre *Film Editing* Richard Marks *Produced by* Sam Spiegel. With Jack Nicholson (Brimmer), Robert De Niro (Monroe Stahr), Tony Curtis (Rodriguez), Robert Mitchum (Pat Brady), Jeanne Moreau (Didi), Donald Pleasence (Boxley).

1978

Goin' South

Directed by Jack Nicholson *Screenplay* John Herman Shaner, Al Ramrus, Charles Shyer, and Alan Mandel, based on a story by John Herman Shaner and Al Ramrus *Cinematography* Nestor Almendros *Original Music* Perry Botkin Jr. and Van Dyke Parks *Film Editing* John Fitzgerald Beck and Richard Chew *Produced by* Harry Gittes and Harold Schneider. With Jack Nicholson (Henry Lloyd Moon), Mary Steenburgen (Julia Tate Moon), Christopher Lloyd (Deputy Towfield), John Belushi (Deputy Hector), Richard Bradford (Sheriff Andrew Kyle), Veronica Cartwright (Hermine).

1980

The Shining

Directed by Stanley Kubrick *Screenplay* Stanley Kubrick and Diane Johnson, based on a novel by Stephen King *Cinematography* John Alcott *Original Music* Wendy Carlos and Rachel Elkind *Film Editing* Ray Lovejoy *Produced by* Stanley Kubrick. With Jack Nicholson (Jack Torrance), Shelley Duvall (Wendy Torrance), Danny Lloyd (Danny Torrance), Scatman Crothers (Dick Hallorann), Barry Nelson (Stuart Ullman), Philip Stone (Delbert Grady).

1981

The Postman Always Rings Twice

Directed by Bob Rafelson *Screenplay* David Mamet, based on a novel by James M. Cain *Cinematography* Sven Nykvist *Set Decoration* Robert Gould *Original Music* Michael Small *Film Editing* Graeme Clifford *Produced by* Charles Mulvehill and Bob Rafelson. With Jack Nicholson (Frank Chambers), Jessica Lange (Cora Papadakis), John Colicos

(Nick Papadakis), Michael Lerner (Mr. Katz), John P. Ryan (Kennedy), Anjelica Huston (Madge).

Ragtime

Directed by Miloš Forman *Screenplay* Michael Weller, based on a novel by E. L. Doctorow *Cinematography* Miroslav Ondríček *Original Music* Randy Newman *Film Editing* Anne V. Coates, Antony Gibbs, and Stanley Warnow *Produced by* Dino De Laurentiis. With Jack Nicholson (Pirate at Beach [uncredited]), James Cagney (New York Police Commissioner Rhinelander Waldo), Mary Steenburgen (Mother), Brad Dourif (Younger Brother), Moses Gunn (Booker T. Washington), Elizabeth McGovern (Evelyn Nesbit), Kenneth McMillan (Willie Conklin).

Reds

Directed by Warren Beatty *Screenplay* Warren Beatty and Trevor Griffiths, based on the life and career of John Reed *Cinematography* Vittorio Storaro *Original Music* Stephen Sondheim *Film Editing* Dede Allen and Craig McKay *Produced by* Warren Beatty. With Jack Nicholson (Eugene O'Neill), Warren Beatty (John Reed), Diane Keaton (Louise Bryant), Edward Herrmann (Max Eastman), Jerzy Kosinski (Grigory Zinoviev).

1982
The Border

Directed by Tony Richardson *Screenplay* Deric Washburn, Walon Green, and David Freeman *Cinematography* Ric Waite *Set Decoration* Barbara Krieger and Robert L. Zilliox *Original Music* Ry Cooder and Domingo Samudio *Film Editing* Robert K. Lambert *Produced by* Edgar Bronfman Jr. With Jack Nicholson (Charlie Smith), Harvey Keitel (Cat), Valerie

Perrine (Marcy), Warren Oates (Red), Elpidia Carrillo (Maria), Shannon Wilcox (Savannah).

1983
Terms of Endearment

Directed by James L. Brooks *Screenplay* James L. Brooks, based on a novel by Larry McMurtry *Cinematography* Andrzej Bartkowiak *Set Decoration* Anthony Mondell and Tom Pedigo *Original Music* Michael Gore *Film Editing* Richard Marks *Produced by* James L. Brooks. With Jack Nicholson (Garrett Breedlove), Shirley MacLaine (Aurora Greenway), Debra Winger (Emma Horton), Danny DeVito (Vernon Dahlart), Jeff Daniels (Flap Horton), John Lithgow (Sam Burns).

1985
Prizzi's Honor

Directed by John Huston *Screenplay* Richard Condon and Janet Roach, based on a novel by Richard Condon *Cinematography* Andrzej Bartkowiak *Set Decoration* Bruce Weintraub *Original Music* Alex North *Film Editing* Kaja and Rudi Fehr *Produced by* John Foreman. With Jack Nicholson (Charley Partanna), Kathleen Turner (Irene Walker), Robert Loggia (Eduardo Prizzi), John Randolph (Angelo "Pop" Partanna), William Hickey (Don Corrado Prizzi), Lee Richardson (Dominic Prizzi), Anjelica Huston (Maerose Prizzi).

1986
Heartburn

Directed by Mike Nichols *Screenplay* Nora Ephron, based on her novel *Cinematography* Nestor Almendros *Set Decoration* Susan Bode *Original Music* Carly Simon *Film Editing* Sam O'Steen *Produced by* Robert Greenhut and Mike Nichols. With Jack Nicholson (Mark Forman), Meryl Streep

(Rachel Samstat), Jeff Daniels (Richard), Maureen Stapleton (Vera), Stockard Channing (Julie Siegel), Richard Masur (Arthur Siegel), Catherine O'Hara (Betty), Steven Hill (Harry Samstat).

1987
The Witches of Eastwick

Directed by George Miller *Screenplay* Michael Cristofer, based on a novel by John Updike *Cinematography* Vilmos Zsigmond *Set Decoration* Joe D. Mitchell *Original Music* John Williams *Film Editing* Hubert C. de la Bouillerie and Richard Francis-Bruce *Produced by* Neil Canton, Peter Guber, and Jon Peters. With Jack Nicholson (Daryl Van Horne), Cher (Alexandra Medford), Susan Sarandon (Jane Spofford), Michelle Pfeiffer (Sukie Ridgemont), Veronica Cartwright (Felicia Alden), Richard Jenkins (Clyde Alden).

Broadcast News

Directed by James L. Brooks *Screenplay* James L. Brooks *Cinematography* Michael Ballhaus *Set Decoration* Jane Bogart *Original Music* Bill Conti *Film Editing* Richard Marks *Produced by* James L. Brooks. With Jack Nicholson (Bill Rorish), William Hurt (Tom Grunick), Albert Brooks (Aaron Altman), Holly Hunter (Jane Craig), Robert Prosky (Ernie Merriman), Lois Chiles (Jennifer Mack), Joan Cusack (Blair Litton).

Ironweed

Directed by Hector Babenco *Screenplay* William Kennedy, based on his novel *Cinematography* Lauro Escorel *Set Decoration* Leslie A. Pope *Original Music* John Morris *Film Editing* Anne Goursaud *Produced by* Keith Barish and Marcia Nasatir. With Jack Nicholson (Francis Phelan), Meryl Streep (Helen Archer), Carroll Baker (Annie Phelan), Michael

O'Keefe (Billy Phelan), Diane Venora (Margaret "Peg" Phelan), Tom Waits (Rudy).

1989
Batman

Directed by Tim Burton *Screenplay* Sam Hamm and Warren Skaaren, based on a story by Sam Hamm and characters by Bob Kane *Cinematography* Roger Pratt *Set Decoration* Peter Young *Original Music* Danny Elfman *Film Editing* Ray Lovejoy *Produced by* Peter Guber and Jon Peters. With Jack Nicholson (Joker/Jack Napier), Michael Keaton (Batman/Bruce Wayne), Kim Basinger (Vicki Vale), Robert Wuhl (Alexander Knox), Pat Hingle (Commissioner James Gordon), Jack Palance (Carl Grissom), Jerry Hall (Alicia Hunt).

1990
The Two Jakes

Directed by Jack Nicholson *Screenplay* Robert Towne, based on his characters *Cinematography* Vilmos Zsigmond *Set Decoration* Jerry Wunderlich *Original Music* Van Dyke Parks *Film Editing* Anne Goursaud *Produced by* Robert Evans, Harold Schneider, and Jack Nicholson (uncredited). With Jack Nicholson (J. J. "Jake" Gittes), Harvey Keitel (Julius "Jake" Berman), Meg Tilly (Kitty Berman), Madeleine Stowe (Lillian Bodine), Eli Wallach (Cotton Weinberger), Rubén Blades (Michael "Mickey Nice" Weisskopf), Frederic Forrest (Chuck Newty).

1992
Man Trouble

Directed by Bob Rafelson *Screenplay* Carole Eastman *Cinematography* Stephen H. Burum *Set Decoration* Samara Schaffer *Original Music* Georges Delerue *Film Editing* William Steinkamp *Produced by* Carole Eastman and Bruce Gilbert. With Jack Nicholson

(Eugene Earl Axline, a.k.a. Harry Bliss), Ellen Barkin (Joan Spruance), Harry Dean Stanton (Redmond Layls), Beverly D'Angelo (Andy Ellerman), Michael McKean (Eddy Revere).

A Few Good Men
Directed by Rob Reiner *Screenplay* Aaron Sorkin, based on his play *Cinematography* Robert Richardson *Set Decoration* Michael Taylor *Original Music* Marc Shaiman *Film Editing* Robert Leighton and Steven Nevius *Produced by* David Brown, Rob Reiner, and Andrew Scheinman. With Jack Nicholson (Col. Nathan R. Jessep), Tom Cruise (Lt. Daniel Kaffee), Demi Moore (Lt. Cmdr. JoAnne Galloway), Kevin Bacon (Capt. Jack Ross), Kiefer Sutherland (Lt. Jonathan Kendrick), Kevin Pollak (Lt. Sam Weinberg), J. T. Walsh (Lt. Col. Matthew Andrew Markinson), James Marshall (Pfc. Louden Downey), Wolfgang Bodison (Lance Cpl. Harold W. Dawson), Michael DeLorenzo (Pfc. William T. Santiago).

Hoffa
Directed by Danny DeVito *Screenplay* David Mamet *Cinematography* Stephen H. Burum *Set Decoration* Brian Savegar *Original Music* David Newman *Film Editing* Lynzee Klingman and Ronald Roose *Produced by* Caldecot Chubb, Danny DeVito, and Edward R. Pressman. With Jack Nicholson (James R. "Jimmy" Hoffa), Danny DeVito (Bobby Ciaro), Armand Assante (Carol D'Allesandro), J. T. Walsh (Frank Fitzsimmons), John C. Reilly (Pete Connelly), Kevin Anderson (Robert Kennedy).

1994
Wolf
Directed by Mike Nichols *Screenplay* Jim Harrison and Wesley Strick

Cinematography Giuseppe Rotunno *Set Decoration* Linda DeScenna *Original Music* Ennio Morricone *Film Editing* Sam O'Steen *Produced by* Douglas Wick. With Jack Nicholson (Will Randall), Michelle Pfeiffer (Laura Alden), James Spader (Stewart Swinton), Kate Nelligan (Charlotte Randall), Richard Jenkins (Detective Bridger), Christopher Plummer (Raymond Alden).

1995
The Crossing Guard
Directed by Sean Penn *Screenplay* Sean Penn *Cinematography* Vilmos Zsigmond *Set Decoration* Derek R. Hill *Original Music* Jack Nitzsche *Film Editing* Jay Cassidy *Produced by* David Hamburger and Sean Penn. With Jack Nicholson (Freddy Gale), David Morse (John Booth), Anjelica Huston (Mary), Robin Wright (Jojo), Piper Laurie (Helen Booth), Richard Bradford (Stuart Booth).

1996
The Evening Star
Directed by Robert Harling *Screenplay* Robert Harling, based on a novel by Larry McMurtry *Cinematography* Don Burgess *Set Decoration* Rick Simpson *Original Music* William Ross *Film Editing* David Moritz and Priscilla Nedd-Friendly *Produced by* David Kirkpatrick, Polly Platt, and Keith Samples. With Jack Nicholson (Garrett Breedlove), Shirley MacLaine (Aurora Greenway), Bill Paxton (Jerry Bruckner), Juliette Lewis (Melanie Horton), Miranda Richardson (Patsy Carpenter).

Mars Attacks!
Directed by Tim Burton *Screenplay* Jonathan Gems, based on a screen story by Jonathan Gems and on trading card series by Topps *Cinematography* Peter Suschitzky *Set Decoration*

Nancy Haigh *Original Music* Danny Elfman *Film Editing* Chris Lebenzon *Produced by* Tim Burton and Larry J. Franco. With Jack Nicholson (President James Dale/Art Land), Glenn Close (First Lady Marsha Dale), Annette Bening (Barbara Land), Pierce Brosnan (Professor Donald Kessler), Danny DeVito (Rude gambler), Natalie Portman (Taffy Dale).

Blood and Wine
Directed by Bob Rafelson *Screenplay* Nick Villiers and Alison Cross, based on a story by Nick Villiers and Bob Rafelson *Cinematography* Newton Thomas Sigel *Set Decoration* William Kemper Wright *Original Music* Michal Lorenc *Film Editing* Steven Cohen *Produced by* Jeremy Thomas. With Jack Nicholson (Alex Gates), Stephen Dorff (Jason), Jennifer Lopez (Gabriela "Gabby"), Judy Davis (Suzanne), Michael Caine (Victor "Vic" Spansky), Harold Perrineau (Henry).

1997
As Good As It Gets
Directed by James L. Brooks *Screenplay* Mark Andrus and James L. Brooks, based on a story by Mark Andrus *Cinematography* John Bailey *Set Decoration* Clay A. Griffith *Original Music* Hans Zimmer *Film Editing* Richard Marks *Produced by* James L. Brooks, Bridget Johnson, and Kristi Zea. With Jack Nicholson (Melvin Udall), Helen Hunt (Carol Connelly), Greg Kinnear (Simon Bishop), Cuba Gooding Jr. (Frank Sachs), Skeet Ulrich (Vincent).

2001
The Pledge
Directed by Sean Penn *Screenplay* Jerzy Kromolowski and Mary Olson-Kromolowski, based on a novel by Friedrich Dürrenmatt *Cinematography*

Chris Menges *Set Decoration* Lesley Beale *Original Music* Klaus Badelt and Hans Zimmer *Film Editing* Jay Cassidy *Produced by* Michael Fitzgerald, Sean Penn, and Elie Samaha. With Jack Nicholson (Jerry Black), Patricia Clarkson (Margaret Larsen), Robin Wright (Lori), Benicio Del Toro (Toby Jay Wadenah), Aaron Eckhart (Stan Krolak), Sam Shepard (Eric Pollack).

2002
About Schmidt
Directed by Alexander Payne *Screenplay* Alexander Payne and Jim Taylor, based on a novel by Louis Begley *Cinematography* James Glennon *Set Decoration* Teresa Visinare *Original Music* Rolfe Kent *Film Editing* Kevin Tent *Produced by* Michael Besman and Harry Gittes. With Jack Nicholson (Warren Schmidt), Kathy Bates (Roberta Hertzel), Hope Davis (Jeannie Schmidt), Dermot Mulroney (Randall Hertzel), June Squibb (Helen Schmidt), Howard Hesseman (Larry Hertzel), Harry Groener (John Rusk).

2003
Anger Management
Directed by Peter Segal *Screenplay* David Dorfman *Cinematography* Donald McAlpine *Set Decoration* Chris L. Spellman *Original Music* Teddy Castellucci *Film Editing* Jeff Gourson *Produced by* Barry Bernardi and Jack Giarraputo. With Jack Nicholson (Dr. Buddy Rydell), Adam Sandler (Dave Buznik), Marisa Tomei (Linda), Luis Guzmán (Lou), Allen Covert (Andrew).

Something's Gotta Give
Directed by Nancy Meyers *Screenplay* Nancy Meyers *Cinematography* Michael Ballhaus *Set Decoration* Beth A. Rubino *Original Music* Hans Zimmer *Film*

Editing Joe Hutshing
Produced by Bruce A.
Block and Nancy Meyers
(uncredited). With Jack
Nicholson (Harry Sanborn),
Diane Keaton (Erica Barry),
Keanu Reeves (Dr. Julian
Mercer), Frances McDormand
(Zoe), Amanda Peet (Marin).

2006
The Departed
Directed by Martin Scorsese
Screenplay William Monahan,
based on a screenplay
written by Alan Mak and
Felix Chong *Cinematography*
Michael Ballhaus *Set
Decoration* Leslie E. Rollins
Original Music Howard
Shore *Film Editing* Thelma
Schoonmaker *Produced
by* Brad Grey, Graham King,
and Brad Pitt. With Jack
Nicholson (Frank Costello),
Leonardo DiCaprio (Billy
Costigan), Matt Damon
(Colin Sullivan), Mark
Wahlberg (Dignam), Martin
Sheen (Oliver Queenan),
Ray Winstone (Mr. French),
Vera Farmiga (Madolyn),
Anthony Anderson (Brown).

2007
The Bucket List
Directed by Rob Reiner
Screenplay Justin Zackham
Cinematography John
Schwartzman *Set Decoration*
Robert Greenfield *Original
Music* Marc Shaiman *Film
Editing* Robert Leighton
Produced by Alan Greisman,
Neil Meron, Rob Reiner,
and Craig Zadan. With Jack
Nicholson (Edward Cole),
Morgan Freeman (Carter
Chambers), Sean Hayes
(Thomas), Beverly Todd
(Virginia Chambers),
Rob Morrow (Dr. Hollins).

2010
How Do You Know
Directed by James L. Brooks
Screenplay James L. Brooks
Cinematography Janusz
Kaminski *Set Decoration*
Merideth Boswell and Nancy
Nye *Original Music* Hans
Zimmer *Film Editing* Richard

Marks and Tracey Wadmore-
Smith *Produced by*
Julie Ansell, James L.
Brooks, Laurence Mark,
and Paula Weinstein. With
Jack Nicholson (Charles
Madison), Reese Witherspoon
(Lisa Jorgenson), Paul Rudd
(George Madison), Owen
Wilson (Matty Reynolds),
Kathryn Hahn (Annie),
Mark Linn-Baker (Ron).

Bibliography

Articles

"Nicholson & Del Toro: Two Reasons to Go to the Movies Talk About Their Crazy Business," *Interview*, November 2002.

Chicago Review, Vol. 33, No. 1, University of Chicago, Summer 1981.

Jeff Giles and David Ansen, "About Jack," *Newsweek*, December 16, 2002.

Patrick Goldstein, "Forever Original—If Not Forever Young," *Los Angeles Times*, February 12, 2003.

Jeff Greenfield, "*Easy Rider*: A Turning Point in Film? A Profound Social Message? An Endless Bummer?," *Esquire*, July 1981.

Diane Johnson, "Stanley Kubrick (1928–1999)," *The New York Review of Books*, April 22, 1999.

Dana Kennedy, "Being Jack," *The Guardian*, October 3, 2002.

Dave Pirie and Chris Petit, "*One Flew Over the Cuckoo's Nest*," *Time Out*, February 20–26, 1976.

Tom Provenzano, "The Star Power Here Is As Good As It Gets," *Drama-Logue*, December 18–31, 1997.

Rex Reed, "The Man Who Walked Off With *Easy Rider*," *The New York Times*, March 1, 1970.

Ron Rosenbaum, "The Creative Mind; Acting: The Method and Mystique of Jack Nicholson," *The New York Times Magazine*, July 13, 1986.

Mike Sager, "Jack Nicholson, 66," *Esquire*, January 2004.

Julian Schnabel, "Jack Nicholson," *Interview*, April 2003.

Fred Schruers, "The *Rolling Stone* Interview: Jack Nicholson," *Rolling Stone*, August 14, 1986.

David Sheff, "*Playboy* Interview: Jack Nicholson," *Playboy*, January 2004.

Mark Singer, "Whose Movie Is This?," *The New Yorker*, June 22, 1998.

Mark Steensland, "*The Shining* Adapted: An Interview with Diane Johnson," *Kamera*, No. 2, March 5, 2012.

James Sterngold, "A Happily Baffled Director Lets His Cast Find Its Own Way," *The New York Times*, December 8, 1997.

Beverly Walker, "The Bird Is On His Own," *Film Comment*, June 1985.

James Wolcott, "Still Cuckoo After All These Years," *Vanity Fair*, December 2011.

Books

Stella Adler and Howard Kissel, *The Art of Acting*, Applause Books, 2000.

Antoine de Baecque, *Tim Burton*, Cahiers du cinéma, 2005.

Cynthia Baron and Sharon Marie Carnicke, *Reframing Screen Performance*, The University of Michigan Press, 2008.

Michael Chekhov, *On the Technique of Acting*, Harper Books, 1991.

Uta Hagen and Haskel Frankel, *Respect for Acting*, John Wiley & Sons, Inc., 1972.

Lee Hill, *Easy Rider*, BFI Publishing, 1996.

Janet Hirschenson, Jane Jenkins, and Rachel Kranz, *A Star Is Found: Our Adventures Casting Some of Hollywood's Biggest Movies*, A Harvest Book - Harcourt, Inc., 2007.

Andrew Klevan, *Film Performance: From Achievement to Appreciation*, Wallflower Press, 2005.

Patrick McGilligan, *Jack's Life: A Biography of Jack Nicholson*, W.W. Norton & Company, 1994.

James Naremore, *Acting in the Cinema*, University of California Press, 1988.

Others

America Lost and Found: The BBS Story (Head/Easy Rider/Five Easy Pieces/Drive, He Said/A Safe Place/The Last Picture Show/The King of Marvin Gardens), DVD, Criterion Collection, 2010.

Vivian Kubrick, "Making *The Shining*," 1980.

Rebecca Murray and Fred Topel, "Jack Nicholson Talks About 'About Schmidt'," www.about.com, December 13, 2002.

Alex Simon, "Forget it, Bob, It's Chinatown: Robert Towne Looks Back on *Chinatown's* 35th Anniversary," *The Hollywood Interview*, November 5, 2009.

1 Fred Schruers, "The Rolling Stone Interview: Jack Nicholson," *Rolling Stone*, August 14, 1986.

2 Pauline Kael, "Nicholson's High," *The New Yorker*, February 11, 1974.

3 Bob Rafelson, e-mail correspondence with the author, January 29, 2013.

4 Mike Sager, "Jack Nicholson, 66," *Esquire*, January 2004.

5 Patrick Goldstein, "Forever an Original— If Not Forever Young," *Los Angeles Times*, February 12, 2003.

6 David Sheff, "Playboy Interview: Jack Nicholson," *Playboy*, January 2004.

7 Fred Schruers, *op. cit.* (see note 1).

8 Monte Hellman, interview with the author, November 14, 2011.

9 Martin Landau, interview with the author, December 6, 2012.

10 Monte Hellman, *op. cit.* (see note 8).

11 Beverly Walker, "The Bird Is On His Own," *Film Comment*, June 1985. Fred Roos, a prominent casting director, won an Academy Award for coproducing *The Godfather Part II* (1974) and was nominated for *Apocalypse Now* (1979). He coproduced *Flight to Fury* and *Back Door to Hell* and was associated with *Drive, He Said, Five Easy Pieces,* and other Nicholson films.

12 Fred Roos, interview with the author, May 6, 2012.

13 Uta Hagen, with Haskel Frankel, *Respect for Acting*, Macmillan, 1973.

14 Erving Goffman, *The Presentation of Self in Everyday Life*, Anchor Books, 1959.

15 Mike Sager, *op. cit.* (see note 4).

16 *Carnal Knowledge* (1971), *The Fortune* (1975), *Heartburn* (1986), *Wolf* (1994).

17 Fred Schruers, *op. cit.* (see note 1).

18 Mac, "Batman," *Variety*, June 14, 1989.

19 Stanley Kauffmann, "About Nicholson," *New Republic*, January 13, 2003.

20 Schneider's dictum is related by Dennis Hopper in a documentary that is part of *America Lost and Found: The BBS Story (Head/Easy Rider/ Five Easy Pieces/Drive, He Said/A Safe Place/ The Last Picture Show/ The King of Marvin Gardens)*, DVD, Criterion Collection, 2010.

21 Rex Reed, "The Man Who Walked Off with *Easy Rider*," *The New York Times*, March 1, 1970.

22 Beverly Walker, *op. cit.* (see note 11).

23 *America Lost and Found, op. cit.* (see note 20).

24 Vincent Canby, "'Easy Rider': A Statement on Film," *The New York Times*, July 15, 1969.

25 Beverly Walker, *op. cit.* (see note 11).

26 Patrick McGilligan, *Jack's Life: A Biography of Jack Nicholson*, W. W. Norton & Company, 1994, p. 21.

27 Lee Hill, "Terry Southern: Ultrahip" in Patrick McGilligan, *Backstory 3: Interviews with Screenwriters of the 60s*, University of California Press, 1997, p. 388.

28 "Hopper [...] told Jay Leno during a 1994 'Tonight Show' appearance that Torn lost the part of booze-addled lawyer George Hanson after pulling a knife on him. [...] Hopper said on the show that Torn attacked him over script changes. But other eyewitnesses identified Hopper, decked out in buckskin, as the knife-wielder. Peter Fonda recalled the two going at each other with a butter knife and a salad fork, according to court records. Hopper's 'Tonight Show' anecdote is false and he knew it, the 2nd District Court of Appeal ruled. A three-judge panel upheld a $475,000 award to Torn, who had sued Hopper for defamation. And the judges rules that Torn could take Hopper back to court for punitive damages." See Ann W. O'Neill, "No Easy Ride for Hopper Over Rip Torn's Lawsuit," *Los Angeles Times*, April 5, 1998.)

29 *America Lost and Found, op. cit.* (see note 20).

30 Conversation with the author, March 2013.

31 Southern volunteered his services to Fonda in the autumn of 1967 when the film was still a pitch. He then wrote a treatment and two drafts in the winter of 1967–1968, copies of which can be found in the New York Public Library and British Film Institute archives. During postproduction, Southern agreed to share the writing credit with Peter Fonda and Dennis Hopper, per the request of Fonda, who asked him to intercede with the Writers Guild to make this happen. Southern's compensation was an estimated $3,500—Writers Guild scale—minus any profit participation. Southern's on-set participation is documented by Karen Black and László Kovács in Nick Jones's documentary *Born to Be Wild*, available on the Criterion DVD.

32 Beverly Walker, *op. cit.* (see note 11).

33 Jeff Greenfield, "*Easy Rider*: A Turning Point in Film? A Profound Social Message? An Endless Bummer?" *Esquire*, July 1981.

34 Roger Ebert, "Five Easy Pieces (1970)," *Chicago Sun-Times*, March 16, 2003.

35 Bob Rafelson, e-mail correspondence with the author, December 10, 2012.

36 *Ibid.*

37 Beverly Walker, *op. cit.* (see note 11).

38 *Ibid.*

39 Rafelson e-mail, *op. cit.* (see note 35).

40 *Ibid.*

41 *America Lost and Found*, *op. cit.*

42 Rafelson e-mail, *op. cit.*

43 *America Lost and Found*, *op. cit.* (see note 20).

44 Bob Rafelson, e-mail correspondence with the author, February 24, 2013.

45 *Ibid.*

46 Ron Rosenbaum, "The Creative Mind; Acting: The Method and Mystique of Jack Nicholson," *The New York Times Magazine*, July 13, 1986.

47 *America Lost and Found*, *op. cit.* (see note 20).

48 Bob Rafelson, e-mail correspondence with the author, December 12, 2012.

49 Alex Simon, "Forget It Bob, It's Chinatown: Robert Towne Looks Back on *Chinatown*'s 35th Anniversary," *The Hollywood Interview*, November 5, 2009. Accessible at http://thehollywoodinterview.blogspot.de/2009/10/robert-towne-hollywood-interview.html.

50 Mark Graves, "Film Guide to *Chinatown*," SUNY Fredonia online, May 9, 2002. Accessible at http://www.fredonia.edu/department/english/shokoff/Chinatown.htm.

51 Beverly Walker, *op. cit.* (see note 11).

52 See the American Film Institute interview "Roman Polanski: Shooting *Chinatown* from Jake Gittes' POV." Accessible at www.youtube.com/watch?v=SAhUliCF6ws.

53 A second film, *The Two Jakes*, directed by and starring Jack Nicholson along with Harvey Keitel and Meg Tilly, was made in 1990.

54 Alex Simon, *op. cit.* (see note 49).

55 Carey McWilliams, *Southern California Country: An Island on the Land*, Duell, Sloan & Pearce, 1946. Reprinted as *Southern California: An Island on the Land*, Peregrine Smith, 1973.

56 Alex Simon, *op. cit.* (see note 49).

57 *Ibid.*

58 Andrew Sarris, *The American Cinema: Directors and Directions, 1928–1968*, Da Capo Press, 1996, p. 151.

59 Release of *Chinatown*, special features, DVD, Paramount Pictures, 2006.

60 Faye Dunaway, *Looking for Gatsby: My Life*, Pocket Books, 1998, pp. 254–255.

61 See the American Film Institute interview "Roman Polanski: *Chinatown* Is a Truly Tragic Story." Accessible at www.youtube.com/watch?v=-ExA-yeWmYE.

62 Vincent Canby, "*Chinatown*," *The New York Times*, June 21, 1974.

63 Beth Ann Krier, "A Costume Designer for the Famous," *Los Angeles Times*, August 4, 1974.

64 Faye Dunaway, *op. cit.* (see note 60), pp. 251 and 255.

65 Richard Ballard, "Roman Polanski," *Penthouse*, August 1974.

66 James Wolcott, "Still *Cuckoo* After All These Years," *Vanity Fair*, December 2011.

67 *Ibid.*

68 Robert Faggen, "Ken Kesey, The Art of Fiction No. 136," *The Paris Review*, Spring 1994.

69 In *Michael Douglas: A Biography*, Marc Eliot states it was actually Kirk Douglas who discovered Miloš Forman on a State Department tour in 1966. While in Czechoslovakia, he saw *Loves of a Blonde* and *The Firemen's Ball* and met Forman. Kirk sent Kesey's book to Forman; however, he never received it. When Michael combed through his father's files, he found the records and contacted Forman, who by then lived in the US. See Marc Eliot, *Michael Douglas: A Biography*, Crown Archetype, 2012, pp. 75–77.

70 Beverly Walker, "Cuckoo's Nest," *Sight & Sound*, Fall 1975, p. 216.

71 Marc Eliot, *op. cit.*, (see note 69) p. 85.

72 Dave Pirie and Chris Petit, "One Flew Over the Cuckoo's Nest," *Time Out*, February 20–26, 1976.

73 *Ibid.*

74 Ron Rosenbaum, *op. cit.* (see note 46)

75 Several of the film's "unknown" actors went on to major careers, most prominently Christopher Lloyd and Danny DeVito. Both were stars of the hit TV series *Taxi* (1978–1983). Lloyd starred in many features, including *Back to the Future* (1985), and DeVito in *Romancing the Stone* (1984). DeVito directed *The War of the Roses* (1989) and produced *Pulp Fiction* (1994), among many other pictures.

76 Edwin Miller, "No Ego in His Act," *Seventeen*, April 1976.

77 Beverly Walker, *Film Comment, op. cit.* (see note 11).

78 Ron Rosenbaum, *op. cit.* (see note 46)

79 Larry McCaffery, "Talking About *The Shining* with Diane Johnson," *Chicago Review*, Vol. 33, No. 1, 1981.

80 Aljean Harmetz, "Kubrick Films 'The Shining' in Secrecy in English Studio," *The New York Times*, November 6, 1978. Accessible online at http://partners.nytimes.com/library/film/110678kubrick-shining.html.

81 Jack Kroll, "Stanley Kubrick's Horror Show," *Newsweek*, June 2, 1980.

82 Robert Emmett Ginna, "The Artist Speaks for Himself," *Entertainment Weekly*, April 9, 1999.

83 Mark Steensland, "The Shining Adapted: An Interview with Diane Johnson," *Kamera*, No. 2, 5 mars 2012. Accessible at http://www.terrortrap.com/interviews/dianejohnson.

84 The set was being constructed as the script was written.

85 Larry McCaffery, *op. cit.* (see note 79)

86 Beverly Walker, *Film Comment, op. cit.* (see note 11).

87 Pauline Kael, "Devolution," *The New Yorker*, June 9, 1980.

88 Gary Don Rhodes, "The Shining," in *Cinematic Hauntings*, Gary J. Svehla, Susan Svehla, ed., Midnight Marquee Press, Inc., 1996, p.279.

89 Diane Johnson, "Stanley Kubrick (1928–1999)," *The New York Review of Books*, April 22, 1999.

90 Vivian Kubrick, behind-the-scenes documentary "Making *The Shining*."

91 *Ibid.*

92 Mac, *op. cit.* (see note 18).

93 "Carnivalesque," a term used by the Russian critic Mikhail Bakhtin, is a mocking or satirical challenge to the traditional social hierarchy. The Feast of Fools, in which lesser figures mock their "betters" and get away with it, is an example; the "Yippies" of the 1960s and 1970s is another.

94 Antoine de Baecque, *Tim Burton*, Cahiers du cinéma, 2011, p. 51.

95 *Ibid.*, p. 50.

96 Beverly Walker, *Film Comment*, *op. cit.* (see note 11).

97 Richard Corliss, "The Caped Crusader Flies Again," *Time*, June 19, 1989.

98 Antoine de Baecque, *op. cit.* (see note 94), p. 48.

99 Richard Corliss, *op. cit.* (see note 97)

100 Kristian Fraga, ed., *Tim Burton: Interviews* (Conversations with Filmmakers), University Press of Mississippi, 1995, p. 26.

101 *Ibid.*, p. 25.

102 Mike Sager, *op. cit.* (see note 4)

103 Richard Corliss, *op. cit.* (see note 97)

104 *Ibid.*

105 Jim Hoberman, "Night and the City," *The Village Voice*, July 4, 1989.

106 The facts were changed. The commander readily admitted authorizing a Code Red, and the Marine being hazed didn't die.

107 Vincent Canby, "Two Marines and Their Code on Trial," *The New York Times*, December 11, 1992.

108 Kenneth Turan, "Two of the Best 'Men,'" *Los Angeles Times*, December 11, 1992.

109 Vivian Kubrick, *op. cit.* (see note 90).

110 Michael Sragow, "Tell It to the Marines," *The New Yorker*, December 14, 1992.

111 Bernard Weinraub, "Rob Reiner's March to 'A Few Good Men,'" *The New York Times*, December 6, 1992.

112 Variation on a line from the theme song written by John Kander and Fred Ebb for Martin Scorsese's *New York, New York* (1977), starring Robert De Niro and Liza Minnelli.

113 Roger Ebert, "*As Good As It Gets*," *Chicago Sun-Times*, December 22, 1997.

114 Dennis Lim, "The Wild Bunch," *The Village Voice*, September 8, 1998.

115 Beverly Walker, *Film Comment, op. cit.* (see note 11).

116 Tom Provenzano, "The Star Power Here Is As Good As It Gets," *Drama-Logue*, December, 18–31, 1997, p. 5.

117 *Ibid.*, p. 6.

118 *Ibid.*

119 Associated Press, "Obsessive-Compulsives Like Jack," March 19, 1998.

120 James Sterngold, "A Happily Baffled Director Lets His Cast Find Its Own Way," *The New York Times*, December 8, 1997.

121 Tom Provenzano, *op. cit.* (see note 116), p. 6.

122 Ed Ochs, "Time Machine," *The Hollywood Reporter*, March 9, 1998, p. C-32.

123 James Sterngold, *op. cit.*

124 Tom Provenzano, *op. cit.*, p. 5.

125 James Sterngold, *op. cit.* (see note 120).

126 Tom Provenzano, *op. cit.* (see note 116), p. 5.

127 Gene Siskel, *TV Guide*, March 21–27, 1998, p. 34.

128 Tom Provenzano, *op.cit.*, p. 6.

129 Tom Provenzano, *op. cit.*, p. 6.

130 The character Nicholson played in *Chinatown* was named after Harry Gittes.

131 Rebecca Murray and Fred Topel, "Jack Nicholson Talks About 'About Schmidt,'" www.about.com, December 13, 2002. Accessible at http://movies.about.com/library/weekly/aaaboutschmidtinta.htm

132 Julian Schnabel, "Jack Nicholson," *Interview* magazine, April 2003.

133 Rebecca Murray and Fred Topel, *op. cit.* (see note 131).

134 Alexander Payne has set three other feature films in Nebraska, the state where he was born and raised: *Citizen Ruth* (1996), *Election* (1999), and *Nebraska* (2013).

135 Richard Schickel, "As Good As He Gets," *Time*, December 16, 2002.

136 Roger Ebert, "*About Schmidt*," *Chicago Sun-Times*, December 20, 2002. Accessible at http://www.rogerebert.com/reviews/about-schmidt-2002.

137 Rebecca Murray and Fred Topel, *op. cit.* (see note 131). Emphasis added.

138 Stephen Holden, "An Uneasy Rider on the Road to Self-Discovery," *The New York Times*, September 27, 2002.

139 Rebecca Murray and Fred Topel, *op. cit.* see note 131).

140 *Ibid.*

141 Dana Kennedy, "Being Jack," *The Guardian*, October 3, 2002.

142 *Ibid.*

143 Louis Begley, *About Schmidt*, Ballantine, 1996, p. 105.

144 Rebecca Murray and Fred Topel, *op. cit.* see note 131).

145 Leo Adam Biga, "About 'About Schmidt': The Shoot, Editing, Working with Jack and the Film After the Cutting Room Floor," *Omaha Weekly*. Accessible at http://leoadambiga.wordpress.com/2011/12/06/from-the-archives-about-about-schmidt-the-shoot-editing-working-with-jack-and-the-film-after-the-cutting-room-floor.

146 Rebecca Murray and Fred Topel, "Kathy Bates Talks About 'About Schmidt,'" www.about.com. Accessible at http://movies.about.com/library/weekly/aaaboutschmidtintb.htm

147 Julian Schnabel, *op. cit.* (see note 132).

148 *Ibid.*

149 Rebecca Murray and Fred Topel, "Jack Nicholson Talks About 'About Schmidt,'" *op. cit.* (see note 146).

150 A. O. Scott, "Weep, and the World Laughs Hysterically," *The New York Times*, December 12, 2003.

151 David Sheff, *op. cit.* (see note 6)

152 *Something's Gotta Give* production notes, Academy of Motion Picture Arts and Sciences.

153 *Ibid.*

154 *Ibid.*

Notes to sidebars

a Mark Singer,
   "Whose Movie Is This?"
   The New Yorker,
   June 22, 1998.

b The actor's other road
   movies are *The Last
   Detail* (1973), *The
   Passenger* (1975), *About
   Schmidt* (2002), and
   The Bucket List (2007).

c Todd Leopold, "'My
   Sister! My Daughter!'
   and Other Tales of
   'Chinatown,'" CNN.
   com, September 29,
   2009. Accessible at
   www.cnn.com/2009/
   SHOWBIZ/
   Movies/09/29/
   chinatown.towne.movie/
   index.html.

d Vincent Canby,
   "*Chinatown*,"
   The New York Times,
   June 21, 1974.

e Alex Simon, *op. cit.*
   (see note 49).

f Robert Siegel, "The
   Making of Chinatown,"
   Blu-ray.com, March 21,
   2012. Accessible at
   http://www.blu-ray.com/
   news/?id=8394.

g Fred Schruers, *op. cit.*
   (see note 1)

h "Nicholson & Del Toro:
   Two Reasons to Go to
   the Movies Talk About
   Their Crazy Business,"
   Interview, November
   2002.

i "Nicholson & Del Toro:
   Two Reasons to Go
   to the Movies Talk
   About Their Crazy
   Business," *Interview*,
   November 2002.

j David Denby, "Scent
   of a woman," *New York*,
   December 14, 1992.

k Sean Macaulay, "Star of
   the Week," *The Times*
   (London), May 17, 2001.

l Author's interview with
   Alexander Payne, April
   2013.

Numbers in *italics* refer to illustrations.

About Schmidt 7, 14, *140*, *141*, *142*, *143*, *144-145*, *146*, *147*, *148-149*, *150*, *151*, *152*, *152*, *153*, 156, 174, 182
Actors Studio 123
Adler, Stella 13, 123
Affair to Remember (An) 155
Andrus, Mark 127, 134, 182
Anger Management 156, 174, 182
Anspach, Susan 42, *44-45*, 156, 179
As Good As It Gets 14, 33, *126*, 127, 128, *128*, 129, *130-131*, *132*, 133, *133*, 134, *135*, *136-137*, 138, *138*, *139*, 156, 174, 182
Astaire, Fred 108
Awful Truth (The) 155
Back Door to Hell 11, 12, 178
Bancroft, Anne 68
Barbera, Joe 11
Basil, Toni 40, *40*
Basinger, Kim *109*, 181
Bates, Kathy *150*, *151*, 182
Batman 7, 14, 81, 96, 98, 99, 100, *101*, *102-103*, 104, *104*, *105*, *106-107*, 108, *108*, *109*, 110, *111*, 123, 156, 173, 181
Begley, Louis 141, 146, 182
Besman, Michael 141, 182
Big Sleep (The) 49, 51, 56, *56*
Black, Karen 33, *36-37*, 38, *40*, 43, 46, 47, 179
Black Peter 66
Bogart, Humphrey 49, 56, *56*, 114, 118, *118*
Brando, Marlon 65, 118, 156, 173, 180
Brecht, Bertolt 123
Broadcast News 128, 173, 181
Brooks, Dean R. (Dr.) 66, 70, 71, 180

Brooks, James L. 127, 128, *128*, *130-131*, 134, *138*, 173, 174, 181, 182, 184
Broussard, Rebecca 174
Bucket List (The) 156, 174, 184
Burton, Tim 11, 99, 100, 104, 108, 110, 128, 173, 174, 181, 182
Cagney, James 9
Caine Mutiny (The) 114, 118, *118*
Carnal Knowledge 33, 63, 82, 173, 179
Carrey, Jim 85, 134
Cassady, Neal 65, 73
Caucasian Chalk Circle (The) 123
Chandler, Raymond 49, 51, 53, 56
Chaplin, Charlie 156
Cher 142, 181
Chinatown 9, 14, 48, 49, *50*, 51, *51*, *52*, 53, *53*, *54-55*, 56, 57, *57*, *58-59*, 60, *60*, 61, 62, 63, 65, 173, 174, 176, 180
Clockwork Orange (A) 97, 110
Columbia Pictures 11, 17, 26
Corey, Jeff 11, 123, 169, 173
Corman, Roger 11, 18, 26, 29, 128, 173, 177, 178, 179
Coward (The) 141
Crothers, Scatman 76, 95, 180
Cruise, Tom 113, 114, *115*, 118, 119, 120, 182
Cry Baby Killer (The) 11, 173, 177
Damon, Matt 156, 184
Davis, Hope 146, *152*, 182
De Niro, Robert 65, 134, 180
Departed (The) 156, 174, *175*, 184
Dern, Bruce 29, 179, 180
DeVito, Danny 72, 180, 181, 182

Devlin, Don 173, 178, 180
DiCaprio, Leonardo 156, 184
Douglas, Kirk 66
Douglas, Michael 66, 67, 180
Dourif, Brad 77, 180, 181
Drive, He Said 7, 53, *170-171*, 173, 179
Dr. Strangelove 97
Dudman, Nick 99, 108
Dunaway, Faye 49, *51*, 57, *57*, 60, 61, 63, 156, 180
Duvall, Shelley 81, 82, *83*, *86-87*, *92-93*, 95, 180
Dylan, Bob 26
Eastman, Carole (a.k.a. Adrien Joyce) 11, 18, 33, 34, 38, 40, 46, 173, 178, 179, 180, 181
Easy Rider 7, 9, 11, 14, 16, 17, 18, *18*, 19, *20-21*, 22, 23, *23*, 24, 25, *25*, 26, *26*, 27, 28, 29, 31, 33, 35, 65, 82, 119, 123, 128, 142, 146, 156, 169, 173, 179
Edward Scissorhands 99
Ed Wood 11
Few Good Men (A) 7, 14, *112*, 113, 114, *114*, *115*, *116-117*, 118, 119, *119*, 120, 121, 122, 123, *124-125*, 174, 182
Fireman's Ball (The) 66
Five Easy Pieces 7, 11, 14, *32*, 33, 34, *34*, 35, *36-37*, 38, 39, *39*, 40, *40*, 41, 42, 43, *44-45*, 46, *46*, 47, 65, 82, 99, 146, 155, 173, 179
Fletcher, Louise 68, 69, 180
Flight to Fury 11, 12, 18, 82, 173, 178
Fonda, Peter 11, 17, 18, *19*, *20-21*, 22, 24, 26, *26*, 29, 31, *31*, 35, 173, 179
Forman, Miloš 66, 68, 78, 79, 180, 181
Forrest Gump 156
Fortune (The) 51, 63, 180
Freeman, Morgan 174, 184
Full Metal Jacket 97

Gaye, Marvin 161
Gielgud, John 85
Gittes, Harry 9, 141, 180, 182
Goffman, Erving 13
Goin' South 173, 180
Gooding, Cuba Jr. 127, 128, *130-131*, 182
Grant, Cary 155
Great Gatsby (The) 53
Hackman, Gene 65, 118
Hagen, Uta 13
Hall, Jerry 100, 181
Hammett, Dashiell 49, 51, 56
Hanks, Tom 156
Hanna, Bill 11
Hawks, Howard 49
Head 11, 18, 34, 173, 179
Hellman, Monte 11, 12, 18, 34, 82, 128, 173, 177, 178, 179
Hoffa 7, 123, 174, *175*, 182
Hoffman, Dustin 65
Hollman, Honey 173
Hollman, Winnie 173
Hopper, Dennis 17, 18, 19, 22, 23, 24, 25, 26, *26*, 29, 31, *31*, 35, 173, 179
How Do You Know 128, 156, 174, *175*, 184
Hunt, Helen 127, 133, *133*, 134, *135*, *136-137*, 138, 156, 174, 182
Hunter, Holly 127, 181
Huston, Anjelica 60, 173, 181, 182
Huston, John 51, 57, *58-59*, 60, 173, 180, 181
Iceman Cometh (The) 97
Ironweed 142, 172, 173, 181
Jenkins, Jane 155
Johnson, Diane 81, 82, 97, 180
Joyce, Adrien *see* Carole Eastman
Kallianiotes, Helena 40, *40*
Kane, Bob 99, 100, 181
Kazan, Elia 123, 180
Keaton, Buster 156
Keaton, Diane 155, 156, *157*,

158, *158*, 160, 161, *162-163*, 166, 174, 181, 184

Keaton, Michael 99, 100, *105*, 110, *111*, 181

Kennedy, Ted 34

Kerouac, Jack 65, 73

Kesey, Ken 65, 66, 73, 79, 180

King, Stephen 81, 180

Kinnear, Greg 127, *130-131*, 134, *135*, 182

Kline, Kevin 127

Knight, Sandra 173, 178

Kovács, Lázsló 23, 25, 179, 180

Kubrick, Stanley 81, 82, 83, 88, *90*, 95, 96, 97, 110, 120, 173, 180

Kubrick, Vivian 85, 97

Ladd, Diane 49, 179, 180

Landau, Martin 11, 123, 169

Lange, Jessica 156, *172*, 180

Lansbury, Angela 68

Larner, Jeremy 173, 179

Last Detail (The) 49, 53, 65, 120, 123, 156, *172*, 173, 180

Laurel and Hardy 156

Lewis, Jerry 85

Little Shop of Horrors (The) 96, 173, 177

Lloyd, Christopher 180

Lloyd, Danny *86-87*, 89, 180

Lloyd, Harold 156

Loves of a Blonde 66

Mad About You 134

McDormand, Frances 155, 156, 184

MacLaine, Shirley 128, 142, 156, 181, 182

Maltese Falcon (The) 49, 56

Man for All Seasons (A) 26

Man Trouble 51, 174, 181

Mars Attacks! 174, 182

Marx Brothers (The) 151

Matinee Theatre 173, 177

Meyers, Nancy 155, 156, *164-165*, 182, 184

Miller, Frank 100

Missouri Breaks (The) 173, 180

Monkees (The) 18, 173

Monkees (The) 11, 18

Monroe, Marilyn 38

Moore, Alan 100

Moore, Demi 113, *115*, 119, 182

Mother Courage and Her Children 123

Mulroney, Dermot 146, 152, 182

Murphy, Eddie 85

Newell, Mike 127

Nichols, Mike 13, 128, 173, 180, 181, 182

Nicholson, Ethel May 8, 9, 173

Nicholson, Jack
 Robert Eroica Dupea 7, 14, 32-47, 173, 179
 J. J. "Jack" Gittes 9, 14, 48-63, 141, 173, 174, 180, 181
 George Hanson 14, 16-31, 35, 173, 179
 Colonel Nathan R. Jessup 14, 112-125, 174, 182
 Randle Patrick McMurphy 14, 64-79, 81, 173, 180
 Jack Napier, a.k.a. The Joker 7, 14, 98-111, 173, 181
 Harry Sanborn 154-167, 184
 Warren Schmidt 7, 140-153, 174, 182
 Jack Torrance 14, 80-97, 173, 180
 Melvin Udall 126-139, 174, 182

Nicholson, Jennifer 9, 151, 173

Nicholson, John Joseph 9, 173

Nicholson, June 8, 9, 173

Nicholson, Lorraine (aunt) 8, 9

Nicholson, Lorraine (daughter) 174

Nicholson, Raymond 174

Oates, Warren 34, 178, 181

Olivier, Laurence 156

One Flew Over the Cuckoo's Nest 14, 64, 65, 66, 66, 67, 68, 69, 70, 71, *71*, 72, *72*, 73, *74-75*, 76, 77, *77*, 78, 79, *79*, 81, 82, 99, 156, 173, *176*, 180

O'Neill, Eugene 65, 97, 173, 181

On the Road 65, 73

Pacino, Al 65

Palance, Jack 104, *104*, 181

Paramount Pictures 53

Payne, Alexander 141, 147, *147*, 151, 174, 182

Peet, Amanda 155, *156*, 184

Penn, Arthur 173, 180

Penn, Sean 128, 182

Perkins, Millie 18, 34, 179

Pfeiffer, Michelle 142, 174, 181, 182

Philadelphia 156

Pledge (The) 7, 182

Polanski, Roman 51, 53, *53*, 57, 63, 173, 180

Ponicsan, Darryl 49, 180

Postman Always Rings Twice (The) 33, 155, *172*, 173, 180

Power, Tyrone 57

Prizzi's Honor 7, 51, 81, 123, 155, 156, 173, *176*, 181

Rafelson, Bob 7, 11, 14, 18, 26, 33, 34, 38, 40, 42, 46, 128, 173, 179, 180, 181, 182

Raven (The) 173, 178

Redfield, William 68, *74-75*, 180

Reeves, Keanu *160*, 161, 184

Reiner, Carl 119

Reiner, Rob *116-117*, 118, 119, 120, 123, 128, 174, 182, 184

Reynolds, Burt 65

Ride in the Whirlwind 11, 13, 18, 173, *176*, 178

Ringwood, Bob 99, 108

Roos, Fred 11, 12, 178

Rosemary's Baby 53

Sampson, Will 68, 69, 78, 180

Sandler, Adam 174, 182

Sarandon, Susan 142, 181

Sartre, Jean-Paul 81

Schneider, Abraham 26

Schneider, Bert 7, 11, 17, 18, 26, 29, 179

Scorsese, Martin 156, 174, 184

Shakespeare, William 113, 141, 146

Shining (The) 7, 14, 33, 80, 81, 82, 83, 84, 85, *86-87*, 88, *88*, 89, *90*, 90, *91*, *92-93*, 94, 95, *95*, 96, 97, *97*, 123, 127, 156, 173, 180

Shooting (The) 11, 18, 34, 82, 173, 178

Smith, George "Shorty" 9

Something's Gotta Give 7, 14, 154, 155, 156, *156*, 157, 158, *158*, *159*, 160, 161, *162-163*, *164-165*, 166, 167, 174, 182

Sorkin, Aaron 119, 182

Southern, Terry 17, 23, 29, 30, 179

Squibb, June 142, *143*, 182

Stanislavski, Constantin 13, 77, 123

Strasberg, Lee 13, 123

Streep, Meryl 142, 181

Sweeney Todd 99

Sylbert, Anthea 57, 63

Sylbert, Richard 57

Taking Off 66

Taylor, Jim 141, 182

Taylor, Robert 57

Terms of Endearment 7, 15, 128, 142, 156, 173, 181

Terror (The) 10, 173, 178

Thin Man (The) 49, 56, 101

Thunder Island 173, 178

To Catch a Thief 155

Torn, Rip 29

Towne, Robert 14, 49, 51, 53, 56, 57, 63, 173, 179, 180, 181

Tracy, Spencer 156

Trip (The) 11, 18, 29, 173, 179

Two Jakes (The) 174, 181

Waite, Ralph 42, 43, 179

Warner Bros. 100, 110

White Heat 9

Witches of Eastwick (The) 7, 81, 96, 100, 123, 142, 156, 173, *175*, 181

Wolf 7, 81, 96, 174, 182

Zaentz, Saul 66, 180

Zwerling, Darrell 49, 180

Original title: *Jack Nicholson*
© 2013 Cahiers du cinéma
SARL

Titre original :
Jack Nicholson © 2013
Cahiers du cinéma SARL

This Edition published by
Phaidon Press Limited
under licence from Cahiers
du cinéma SARL, 65, rue
Montmartre, 75002 Paris,
France © 2013 Cahiers
du cinéma SARL.

Cette Édition est publiée
par Phaidon Press Limited
avec l'autorisation des
Cahiers du cinéma SARL,
65, rue Montmartre,
75002 Paris, France © 2013
Cahiers du cinéma SARL.

Cahiers du cinéma
65, rue Montmartre
75002 Paris

www.cahiersducinema.com

ISBN 978 0 7148 6668 0

A CIP catalogue record
of this book is available from
the British Library.

Series concept designed
by Thomas Mayfried
Designed by Line Célo

Printed in China

Acknowledgments

Bill Krohn persuaded me
to tackle this book and
encouraged me throughout
its arduous journey to
completion. Leonard Klady
and Fred Roos, likewise,
were ever constant with
support and assistance.
I am grateful to Monte
Hellman, Alexander Payne,
Bob Rafelson, and Rob Reiner
for sharing their directorial
experiences, and to Martin
Landau and Bruce Dern for
their unique perspectives.
Lee Hill, Patrick McGilligan,
Mike Kaplan, the film-smart
staff at Cinefile Video, and
casting mavens Jane Jenkins
and Janet Hirshenson were
distinctly helpful.
The Academy of Motion
Picture Arts and Sciences'
Margaret Herrick Library
was an invaluable resource.
Special thanks to the
hardworking Cahiers du
Cinema staff, especially to
Valerie Buffet and Carolina
Lucibello.
This book is dedicated,
in memory, to my own great
acting teachers, William
Hickey, Mira Rostova, and
Fanny Bradshaw, and to Jack
Nicholson himself for the
challenges inherent in his art.

Photographic credits

© 1978 Gary Lewis/mptvimages.com/
Photo Masi: cover; BFI/Columbia Pictures:
pp. 24 (t), 25, 26, 27, 28; BFI/Paramount
Pictures: pp. 48, 51, 53; BFI/New Line
Cinema: pp. 140, 143; Castle Rock Ent./
Columbia Pictures: pp. 115, 121, 122;
Christophel/Columbia Pictures: pp. 20-21;
Christophel/Columbia Pictures/Warner
Bros.: pp. 154, 160 (t, b), 162-163, 167
(t, b); Christophel/Fantasy Films/United
Artists: p. 78; Christophel/New Line
Cinema: p. 147; Christophel/Warner Bros.:
pp. 83 (t, b), 90; Christophel/Warner Bros./
DC Comics Inc.: pp. 108, 111 (b);
Collection BNF/Adrian Barrère: p. 96;
Collection Cinémathèque française/Castle
Rock Ent./Columbia Pictures:
pp. 124-125; Collection Cahiers du
cinéma/Twentieth Century Fox Film
Corporation: p. 175 (tr); Collection
Cahiers du cinéma/A.I. P.: p. 172 (tl);
Collection Cahiers du cinéma/Columbia
Pictures: pp. 32, 34, 36-37, 39 (t, b), 46,
172 (tr), 175 (br); Collection Cahiers du
cinéma/Columbia Tristar Films: pp. 132
(t), 133, 136-137, 138, 172 (br); Collection
Cahiers du cinéma/D.Rabourdin/
Paramount Pictures: pp. 57, 61; Collection
Cahiers du cinéma/D. Rabourdin/Warner
Bros.: p. 97; Collection Cahiers du cinéma/
Fantasy Films/United Artists: pp. 66, 76 (t),
77, 79; Collection Cahiers du cinéma/
Paramount Pictures: pp. 58-59; Collection
Cahiers du cinéma/Proteus Films: p. 13;
Collection Cahiers du cinéma/Warner
Bros.: pp. 56, 88, 89, 95, 175 (tl), 175 (bl);
Collection Cahiers du cinéma/Warner
Bros/DC Comics Inc.: pp. 98, 102-103;
Collection Cat's/Columbia Pictures/
Warner Bros.: pp. 164-165; Collection
Cat's/Columbia Tristar Films: pp. 126,
130-131; Collection Cat's/Paramount
Pictures: pp. 54-55; Collection Cat's/
Warner Bros./DC Comics Inc.: p. 111 (t);
Collection Cinémathèque française/
Columbia Pictures: pp. 18, 19 (t);
Collection Cinémathèque française/
Fantasy Films/United Artists: p. 64;
Collection Cinémathèque française/
Warner Bros.: pp. 80, 86-87; Collection
Margaret Herrick Library/AMPAS/Castle
Rock Ent./Columbia Pictures: p. 112;
Collection Margaret Herrick Library/
AMPAS/Castle Rock Ent./Columbia
Pictures/Sidney Baldwin: pp. 114,
116-117; Collection Margaret Herrick
Library/AMPAS/Columbia Pictures: pp.
16, 170-171; Collection Margaret Herrick
Library/AMPAS/Columbia Tristar Films:
p. 128; Collection Margaret Herrick
Library/AMPAS/Fantasy Films/United
Artists: pp. 67, 69 (t), 71, 72, 76 (b);
Collection Margaret Herrick Library/
AMPAS/Paramount Pictures: pp. 15, 52
(b), 172 (bl); Collection Photo12/Archives
du 7e Art/Columbia Pictures/Warner Bros.:
p. 156; Collection Photo12/Archives du 7e
Art/New Line Cinema: pp. 142, 144-145,
148-149; Collection Photo12/Columbia
Pictures: p. 23; Collection Photo12/
Compagnia Cinematografica Champion/
CIPI/MGM: p. 35; Collection Photo12/
Fantasy Films/United Artists: pp. 69 (b),
176 (bl); Collection Photo12/Paramount
Pictures: p. 176 (tr); Collection Photo12/
Warner Bros.: p. 92-93; Collection
Photo12/Warner Bros/Dc Comics Inc.:
pp. 101 (r), 104, 106-107; Collection
Photofest/ Twentieth Century-Fox
Television: p. 101 (l); Collection Photofest/
Castle Rock Ent./Columbia Pictures:
p. 119; Collection Photofest/Columbia
Pictures: pp. 40, 44-45, 118; Collection
Photofest/Columbia Pictures/Peter Sorel:
pp. 19 (b), 24 (b); Collection Photofest/
Columbia Tristar Films: pp. 132 (b), 139;
Collection Photofest/Paramount Pictures:
pp. 52 (t), 60; Columbia Pictures: pp. 22,
41 (t, b), 43, 47; Columbia Pictures/Warner
Bros.: pp. 157, 158, 159; Columbia Tristar
Films: pp. 129, 135; Fantasy Films/United
Artists: p. 70; Fred Roos Collection: p. 12
(t, b); © Henri Cartier-Bresson/Magnum
Photos: p. 30; Ken Kesey Papers, Ax 279,
box 3/Special Collections and University
Archives,University of Oregon Libraries,
Eugene, Oregon: p. 73; © Lord Snowdon/
CAMERA PRESS/GAMMA: pp. 6; New
Line Cinema: p. 153; Paramount Pictures:
pp. 50, 62; Patrick McGilligan/*Jack's life:
a Biography of Jack Nicholson*/ph:
Jonathan Epaminondas: p. 8 (t); Patrick
McGilligan/*Jack's life: a Biography of Jack
Nicholson*: p. 8 (b); © Rue des Archives/
BCA: p. 31; The Kobal Collection/A.I.P.:
p. 10; The Kobal Collection/Columbia
Pictures: p. 183; The Kobal Collection/
Fantasy Film/United Artists: pp. 74-75;
The Kobal Collection/Proteus Films:
p. 176 (tl); Twentieth Century Fox: p. 176
(br); Warner Bros.: pp. 84, 91, 94; Warner
Bros./DC Comics Inc.: pp. 105, 109.

All reasonable efforts have been made
to trace the copyright holders of the
photographs used in this book.
We apologize to anyone that we were
unable to reach.

Cover illustration
Jack Nicholson in 1978.